Genuine
Blacksmith

David Wilson

Genuine Blacksmith

Mr. David Wilson

To order additional copies of this book, contact:
Xlibris Corporation
1-888-795-4274
www.Xlibris.com
Orders@Xlibris.com
121709

Memoirs of a Legendary Blacksmith:

David Wilson

Born September 23, 1939

PROLOGUE

I want to put in perspective what made me click. My wife, Norma, and I were very young when we got married, and even though I knew I wanted to be a blacksmith, it was hard to get it all together. As time went on, it didn't get any easier. When the kids came along, it was even harder to learn a trade, and make a living. There were many times over the years that I wanted to give up and quit. Norma would say, we have all these kids to feed, and we would talk it out, and the next day things would be better. It wasn't until Norma started training horses that I realized how talented she was with horses. Then, after she took some three-hundred-dollar horses and made nice race horses out of them, I wasn't surprised. She raised our children the same caring way that she took care of the horses. I was never one to say, "I'm sorry" or "I love you", but just knowing that I had someone to take care of us made it so much easier to concentrate on my career as a blacksmith. I don't think I would have made it if it hadn't been for Norma. Thanks everyone, especially my wife and kids, for putting up with me for all these years as a blacksmith because that's not an easy job. I probably stepped on a lot of toes over the years, and I want to thank everyone.

My life started in the small town of Bradfordsville, Kentucky, on September 23rd 1939. I'll get on with the first recollection I have. When I was about five years old, my Mom, Dad, and brother lived on Caney Creek, in Lebanon, Kentucky. That was about the time my sister, Betty Carrol, was born. That's about all I remember, except for the time I almost cut my leg off cutting up kindling. I missed the chopping block, and hit my leg, and almost cut my leg completely off. My mom patched me up. Back those days all women were like doctors. They kept everything on hand to fix cuts and scrapes. Also, lots of hugs and kisses. I healed up OK, even though I still have a scar. There were no emergency rooms then.

In nineteen hundred forty-four we moved about a mile down the road to another farm, the Desari Luckett place. That was the year I turned six and started to school. My brother and I had to walk two miles through the fields to catch the bus. We went all the way to Bradfordsville, which was ten miles. I went to Bradfordsville School my first four years. That was a good experience and headed me in the right direction for the way my life turned out.

The first four years I went to school, my father was a sharecropper. Being so young, I didn't realize we were poor. I remember getting only a cap pistol for Christmas. I only got one pair of shoes a year, and that was when I started to school. I remember having one pair of jeans. My mother would wash them by hand every night and hang them on the line outside until dark, and then she would bring them inside the house to finish drying.

For several years we didn't have electricity. Therefore, we only had an ice box to keep our food from spoiling. We went to town once a week to get necessities, and Daddy would get one block of ice. The ice didn't last very long, so we also had a spring house to put other things in that needed to be kept cool. Things were very different back those days.

My grandfather on my mother's side, Walker Gribbins, lived close to Bradfordsville School. I used to go to his house regularly, and he had something that I was very interested in—horses and horse-shoeing boxes. So every first Sunday, all the family on my mother's side, would get together and go to Papa's. That's what everyone called him.

Spalding Place   David's Grandfather's place where he was raised when he was young.

My grandfather had work horses and he put shoes on them regularly. The first time I saw him shoe a horse it was the most fascinating thing I had ever seen. I loved the smell, and I still do, sixty years later.

Papa had a riding horse named Sue. I was very small, but I felt like a giant when I was riding old Sue.

Sometimes on Friday my aunt Dorothy Jean, who was quite a bit older than me, would meet me at school and we would ride the bus to Papa's. I would spend the whole weekend there. While I was there, Papa would take the horses and wagon to Bradfordsville. Since it was almost three miles, he would saddle up "Old Sue" and let me ride her. He would plow and disk everybody's garden in Bradfordsville, and prepare it for planting. We'd spend a couple of afternoons down there and then I'd ride "Old Sue" back home.

The first Sunday in every month all the family on my mother's side of the family would come to Papa's house and we all had a big feast. I look back now and wonder how my Grandmother cooked for all those people. My mother had four sisters, and them and their families were there, also. It is wonderful to be young. I was just nine, but I felt like I was old enough to vote. One day while we were at Papa's, my cousins, Roger and Randall Cox, and I went back in the woods and cut some long cedar poles and made a wig-wam. We played in it all summer. That fall Papa went back to the wig-wam and it was full of rattlesnakes. Papa had to burn the wig-wam down.

As a child, one of the places I most liked to go, was Uncle John and Aunt Searie Sealey's house. They owned a farm in a community called Green Briar, Kentucky. One of the things I most remember were their Papaw trees. When the papaws got ripe they were delicious. My uncle Walter Sealey and his son Weasley had another project that I didn't like to smell, but was good to eat. They made limburger cheese. They went through a lot of work putting the ingredients together. Then they buried it in the ground for a few weeks. When they took the cheese out of the ground, you can't believe how horrible it smelled, but they would cut the bad part off and have a big block of cheese.

On around the creek, my cousin, Brother Houston, preached at a little Baptist church. Sometimes we, and a lot of our families, would go to church there. I especially remember the Baptizings they would have. There was a big hole of water down below Sealey's farm, and that is what they used for the baptizings. I also remember picking blackberries on the farm, and getting chiggers all over me. I won't forget that if I live to be a hundred years old.

In Nineteen Forty Nine I was ten years old. My dad quit farming and moved to Lebanon, Kentucky. He worked at public work for a while, and my mother worked at a sewing factory. Even back then I was very talented. I started making bed dolls, and my mother would take them to work with her and sell them for three dollars and fifty cents each. Back then that was a lot of money. I made the dolls dress from milk strainer pads and yarn.

We rented a house for a while after we moved to Lebanon, and then my dad built a house at the edge of town. The house was next to a grocery store and close to the city park. I thought that I was in seventh heaven.

By now my little sister was five years old, and we were old enough to stay by ourselves while mom and dad worked. It wasn't long before I got one of my big ideas. We had a big sand pile that was left from building our house. The house wasn't very high, so I made me a parachute to jump off the house, into the sand. The day I decided to jump, the parachute didn't open, and I was lucky I didn't get hurt.

After we moved to Lebanon, Kentucky, I was in a different school district. Right outside of Lebanon a new school had just been built. The school was Glasscock Elementary School. I started to Glasscock school in the fifth grade. The very first thing I saw was this beautiful young girl. My heart hit the window and bounced back. I never saw anything on earth like her. I was in love at age ten, and I am still in love sixty years later. Her name was Norma Jean Gordon.

For the next couple of years, my little sister and I played and fought a little bit and I was getting big enough to mow the lawn. It was hard for me to mow, because the lawnmowers were very heavy back then, and the yard was very rough.

By this time I had gotten some goats. One day, one of the goats jumped out of a lawn chair and broke his leg. My neighbor wanted to cut the goat's throat, but I went next door to the grocery store, picked up some popsicle sticks, made a splint out of them, fixed his leg, and it healed just fine. You couldn't even tell which leg was broken.

About this time, I started thinking about making a goat cart to work my goats to. It took me nearly a month to get the cart made. It was hard to find all the parts that I needed. When I finished the cart I needed some harness, so I went to Beggley's Bicycle Shop. Mr. Beggley was also a leather maker, and he sold me some leather to make the harness.

I started working my goats to their carts regularly, and I had a wonderful time. I didn't know it then, but I was getting valuable blacksmith training.

On day I had my goat hooked up in front of our house, and a car stopped. A man got out of the car and came over to me. I recognized him to be Doctor Campbell, the most famous doctor in Lebanon, Kentucky. Doc asked me if I wanted a goat big enough to ride. I said, "you bet I do", so he took me to his house, and we walked to where the goats were. He had several milk goats, and one giant goat. I knew this was the goat he was talking about. Doc told me to take him home and enjoy riding him. He also gave me a lead rope, and told me to keep it. I led my big goat right through town, and everyone thought he was a small horse, until they took a second look. The goat was well broke. I make him a new bridle, and I rode him everywhere. People started calling me the goat kid. I could either ride the goat or drive him to my cart.

It had been three years since we moved to town, and I was almost twelve years old. I had accomplished a lot for a boy my age. One day my dad asked me if I would like to work in the grocery store next door. I thought that Mrs. Barlow wanted me to work in the store, as she was always wanting me to do something for her. My dad said he was thinking about buying the store. I knew I would like working in the store, but I didn't know if I could keep my goats. I would just have to wait and see. Twelve year olds are not very patient, and in those days, people didn't make quick decisions.

It wasn't long before the Barlow's and my dad made a deal. He traded our house and a little money for the store. There was always several men around the grocery store, and it didn't take them long to move our things to the apartment above the store. My dad would be working there full time.

We had some milk cows on a farm across the road from the store. My dad wanted me to milk them twice a day. He said he would pay me four dollars a week to milk the cows. Back in those days, I knew that I would be rich in no time at all.

I had an old bicycle that my brother had given me, but I needed a new one. Now that I was working, I went to the bicycle shop in town and bought me a new Roadmaster Bike. It had a horn and a light. Boy, I thought that I was rich. I told the owner of the shop that I would pay him two dollars a week until it was paid for, and I did.

I not only milked the cows, but I also worked in the grocery store. By then I was getting big enough to do man sized things. Our neighbor, who lived up the road from us, wanted me to drive the tractor for them on their farm. They had a large farm, and needed someone to drive the tractor and till up the tobacco and corn ground. My neighbor, Mr. Grundy, told me he would pay me two dollars a day, and that I could work every day that I wanted to.

All that summer I worked three or four days a week on the Grundy farm. I also milked the cows twice a day for my dad. There was a doctor in our town who bought milk from us. My mother had a pasteurizer. She would pasteurize his milk and he would pick it up at the store every day.

I worked in the store every day that I could. Daddy mostly wanted me to work on weekends. It was really nice living close to town and the city park.

Back then, most of the town kids went to the movie house every Saturday and Sunday. My mother didn't want me to ride my bicycle at night, so she would give me money for a cab, to and from the movies. It only cost fifty cents each way. Those were wonderful times. I had a lot of little friends, male and female. Since I was working, I always had spending money. I also started swapping some of my things with other people, and made a little money from that. I worked like that all summer.

I was working in the grocery store one day when a man came in and started talking to my father. He introduced himself to me, and wanted to know who I was. My dad told him that I was his son. The man's name was Buford Bradshaw. He said he had a back operation that had left him paralyzed in his back and legs. He said that he was an electrician, and that he was always needing young guys to help him run electric wires in houses that he was working on. That didn't appeal to me much until he said that he would probably have to quit taking care of his horses. I asked what kind of horses that he had, and he said he had some race horses that he run at the fair every year.

I told him not to worry about the horses, that I was a first class boy for the job. Buford said that it wouldn't be long until we started working with the horses, but in the mean time I could help him wire some houses.

Some of us guys started hanging out at the fair grounds, which was only half a mile through the field, to my dad's store. One day Buford wanted to go out to the fair grounds where the horses were stabled, and clean the stalls and bed them down with clean straw. While we were there, a young man came walking up and wanted to know if anyone needed someone to help them work. He said he had just moved there and didn't know anyone. Buford told him if he wanted to work, he could start helping us right then. The man was a good worker, and later I asked him his name. He said his name was Bobby Isham, and that was the beginning of a life time friendship. Several years later, Bobby became a blacksmith, also. For nearly three years, Bobby and I did whatever Buford told us to do. I have to give Papa a lot of credit for getting me involved with the horses, but I have to give Buford a lot of credit, also.

One day my dad told me that the goats had to go. By then Bobby and I were thirteen, and the horses had started to take the place of the goats. Playing with the goats was a wonderful experience, and I will never forget them.

Bobby and I tried to help Buford as much as we could, but we were young, and didn't know much about electricity. Buford was the electrician, and we tried to help him as much as we could, but our love was for the horses. Buford didn't get mad at us so it worked out pretty well.

When it was time to bring the horses in from the fields to train them, it wasn't at all like I thought it would be. The horses were nearly four miles out of town. After we caught them, Buford rode in the truck, and Bobby and I had to lead the horses all the way back to town. We made it, but believe me, it was not easy. It took a few months to get them ready to run, but it was worth it just to get to ride them every day.

I could ride really well from helping Papa all the time, but Bobby didn't have very much experience. But young people learn fast. I was getting excited about going to the fairs with the horses. It took all summer to go to all the fairs. It was a lot of fun.

By this time I had gotten rid of all my goats except one. I kept a young goat named Truman. I had taught Truman to be mean if you picked on him. A lot of people picked at the goats, but you would get a surprise if you picked at Truman. He would knock you down if you touched his horns.

The first day we started to the fair I was very excited. We had a gentleman named Jim Bob Wade to haul the horses on his van. Mr. Wade was Bobby's uncle, and he had one of the fastest ponies in the state. The pony's name was Little Red, and I got to ride her because I was small. Buford took a thoroughbred mare to the fair that was very fast. I rode her a lot and won a lot of races on her. I never dreamed how much I was learning from all this.

The first fair we went to was in Columbia, Kentucky. This was another new experience for us. I guess Bobby and I looked like two loose horses. When we started racing, Little Red won every race that she ran. The thoroughbred mare that Buford brought to the fair won the first day, and was third the last day of the fair. Her name was Crow Mun. Everything that two boys could do, we did.

A few times I took Truman, the goat, to the carnival at night. He would pick up every cigarette butt that he saw, and eat them. He was perfect in a crowd, as long as you didn't touch his horns.

We had only been in Columbia for a week, when I started meeting young people, that later on in life I would work for as a blacksmith. The first two that I met was Roger Burton and Larry Holt, and they have been life long friends ever since. After the fair was over on Saturday, we went back home until the following Tuesday. All the fairs always started on Wednesday.

The next Tuesday we shipped the horses to Russell Springs, Kentucky. Jim Bob Wade took us on his van. Everything was all new again, with different people. Russell Springs was the largest fair in Kentucky in those days. On Wednesday the races started. Little Red won very easy the first day. I rode the thoroughbred mare, and she was third again. The next day, Hulan Wamack asked if I would ride a horse for him. That was another new experience for me. I asked Buford, and he said that he thought it would be OK. He was kind of my guardian at the fairs.

I rode Hulan's horse, and she finished third. He was pleased by the horse and the way that I rode her. Later on that day, someone had a horse with a shoe off. They asked if I knew anyone who could fix it. I told them that I probably could. I got Buford's shoeing tools from his truck and fixed the shoe. Buford had showed me how to drive the nails in the shoe, and that was a good start.

On Wednesday, the last day of the fair, Buford let Bobby ride Crow Mun in a race. That race didn't turn out very well. She bowed the tendon in her leg, and it was pretty bad. Buford called Charley Montgomery, who owned the other half of the mare, and asked what he wanted him to do. Charlie said to bring her home and he would breed her and another mare that he had. Charley Montgomery was the Washington County Attorney, and was one of the nicest people that I ever met. I rode in some of my earlier races with a gentleman named Dravo Foley, who also became a life time friend.

The fairs were a lot of fun, especially at night when the carnival was going on. They had a lot of fun things going on. The fair ended at Russell Springs, and we went back home until Tuesday.

The next week we went to Campbellsville, Kentucky. The fairs don't really change that much, just the people and livestock. This is where I met Jim Maupin. He was a standard bred driver. The standard bred horses run at the fairs back then. He also became a very good friend.

By now there were five of us who hung around the fairs together. Morris Glazebrook was a horse person. His father had some ponies and plug horses. Orville Walls didn't have horses, but he rode races for other people. Roger Thompson's father owned several farms and a lot of horses. We were all friends, but Bobby and I were probably the closest. We went everywhere together.

When the fairs were over for the summer, we still worked around the fair ground. When I started back to school that fall, I still walked through the field each morning to take care of horses, and then I would catch the bus to school. I still worked at my dad's store and milked the cows. I always put in a full day.

There was a gentleman named Sam Burnett, who had standard bred horses, and liked to nip a little at the bottle. Sam had a thirty-nine Chevrolet. On Friday nights, we five boys would buy Sam a half pint of liquor, and he would let us borrow his car. We would go to the river, along with a lot of other kids, and have a good time. There was a taxi driver who would bring us what ever we wanted to drink, we just paid him fifty cents extra for the cab fare.

By now I was fifteen, and I really didn't like school. I was always wanting to learn something about blacksmithing. I would be sixteen in September, and I was thinking in the back of my head about quitting school. It was fall, and people turned their horses out for the winter. I found a job working in a restaurant after school. I really enjoyed working there. A lot of my friends came in to eat.

I didn't have to work on Saturday or Sunday, so Bobby and I would hitch hike to Lexington, Kentucky once in a while. One week-end we went by a leather shop on Broadway, and went inside. We met the owner, Paul Ladd. Paul was a very colorful person, and it seemed like I had known him all my life. After that we visited Paul every time we went to Lexington.

I used to stop by a pawn shop on Upper Street in Lexington to look for horse things. Even though I wasn't very old, I had accumulated a few blacksmith tools, and some horse riding equipment. It was now October, and Keeneland Race Track was getting ready to start the fall meet. I told Bobby we needed to go to Keeneland the next week-end. We went to Keeneland early, stopped by to see Paul Ladd, then went to Phillip Gall's pawn shop. I couldn't believe what I saw. There was a race saddle that had a sixteen dollar, out of pawn, price tag. I bought it and took it straight to Keeneland. I took the saddle to the Jockey's room and sold it to Johney Heckman for one hundred and fifty dollars.

I still had one horse to feed through the winter. I would make enough money doing this to buy hay and grain all winter. I was very lucky. Bobby and I enjoyed going to the races, and we knew lots of race track people before we ever went to work at Keeneland.

One year Buford gave me a horse magazine for Christmas. At the time, it was the highlight of my life. It had lots of horse stories and pictures. My mother had threatened to make me leave home, because my bedroom was covered with horse pictures.

The restaurant where I worked had a pool room in the back. One afternoon I was watching a pool game when a young man, who was playing pool, lost all his money on a pool game. He said he would sell his car for a hundred dollars. I spoke up and said I would give him forty dollars. No one else said anything, so he said he would take it. I bought the car, but I wouldn't be old enough to drive for a couple of months.

Bobby and I had done a lot of things together, and we were talking about quitting school. Bobby was a little younger than I was. He wouldn't be sixteen until January, but I was almost sixteen then. When you are that age, you really don't know what you want to do. I also had to deal with what my dad would say. That wasn't going to be easy. I knew in my heart what I wanted to do, but I knew it would take a long time to become a blacksmith. I felt that if I went to Lexington, I could meet the right people to help me out. I was trying to put things together in my mind.

I was still working at the restaurant and driving my car. It was a nineteen forty-one Chevrolet coupe, and I didn't know how long it would last. One part of me was telling me not to quit school, because one of my teachers told me I should become an architect, another said I should become an artist, but I knew the blacksmith side would win.

One day I went to school, and when the class started, I just couldn't sit there. I got all my things together, told everyone goodbye, and walked down the road. I couldn't keep from crying. I knew that I had walked away from the biggest part of my life.

When I got home, it wasn't as bad as I thought it would be. I know it hurt my dad, because he couldn't understand why I wanted to work with the horses. He told me that I probably wouldn't amount to a hill of beans. That is what he always told me, but I knew that I could do whatever I decided to do with my life.

After things finally settled down, Bobby and I, and the other guys, were still hanging out at the fair grounds. I didn't do much until Christmas, so that gave me a chance to do some things in the house for my mother that she had been wanting me to do. I felt good about helping her.

On January second, nineteen-fifty-six I went to Keeneland Race Track and asked around about a job. Some man told me to go to barn sixteen and ask for Eddie Anspach. I went to the barn, and there Mr. Eddie stood. I introduced myself and told him that I was looking for a job. He said he had some horses turned out on the farm, and he would be bringing them to Keeneland on January fifth, and I could start to work on that day. I told him that I didn't have a lot of experience, but I had been riding at the fairs, and galloping horses at home for Mr. Bradshaw.

I went back home, and as soon as I got back, I run into a man named Paul Willard. He raised standard breds, but said that he had a thoroughbred yearling for sale. I didn't need a yearling horse, but I knew where I could sell him. The next day I drove to Perville, Kentucky. I knew J. H. Webb. I saw his father first, and told him I had a horse for sale. He asked me if I would trade the horse for his old car. I looked at the car, and it looked new, but it was a thirty-one Plymouth. He said that there was something wrong with the car. You could be driving down the road in it, and it would just stop running. I told Mr. Webb that I would trade the horse for the car.

I started home in the car, and about halfway home it quit running. I reached down and shook the key and it started running again. When I got home I took it to Pickrell's Garage, they put a new switch on it, and it was as good as new. I needed a good car when I started to work at Keeneland. The only other thing it needed was tires, so I had some big tires and rims put on, and I was tickled to death. It would only run seventy miles an hour, but that was plenty fast enough, back in the those days.

On January the fifteenth, nineteen fifty six, I went to work for Edwin Anspach. Right away he told me to call him "Mr. Eddie", and that is what I called him for the rest of the years that I knew him. After I started working, I went by Pinkston's Turf Shop to see Paul Ladd. I asked him if he knew where I might rent a room to live in. He told me there was some rooms to rent out by the trotting track, which was out on West Broadway. He said these rooms were close to Keeneland. I drove out to the area he had told me about, and went to the house and knocked on the door. An older lady came to the door, and I asked if she had a room for rent. She told me no, that they were in a house up the street. I thanked her and started to leave. She said, wait a minute, come in and sit down, my lunch is almost ready. She said, you know, my daughter lives here, and she is never home. It might be nice to have a young man for company, so she made me eat lunch with her. She said, I am so excited that I forget to tell you my name, it is Mrs. Rodgers. She said that her husband had been dead for a long time.

I asked how much the room rented for, and she said she would wait and ask her daughter when she came home later that day. Mrs. Rodgers told me to bring my clothes in out of the car, and she showed me where my room and the bathroom was. There weren't many regulations there. She said that she didn't sleep much anyway, so me coming in and out of the house wouldn't bother her. She said that she had two grandsons that would be coming by every once in a while. Their names were Chris and Bobby.

When Mrs. Rodgers daughter got home they talked, and then they called me into the kitchen. Mrs. Rodgers introduced her daughter, and told me she would fix a light lunch, and cook a big supper every night for fifteen dollars a week. I couldn't believe I had found a place like that.

Mr. Eddie started my salary at sixty dollars a week, so if I was careful, I could make it. I lived there until the next spring, and I went with Bobby and Chris a lot. They were very good people.

I really enjoyed working for Mr. Eddie. He took me into his life, and treated me like the son he never had. I didn't realize it, but I had learned more at the fairs than I thought. I watched the other exercise boys, and I did fine. Mr. Eddie started showing me how to feed the horses, and how to look for trouble, and how to take their temperatures. It takes all that to make a good horse person.

As time went by, I met some blacksmiths at the race track. When I told them I wanted to be a blacksmith, they would tell me that I should do something else. After I had worked at Keeneland for a while, I started hanging out at Pinkston's Turf Shop two or three afternoons a week. Paul and I hit it off well. I started making little things out of leather, and helping Paul sweep the floor before closing at night. Morris, who worked for Paul, was into hand tooling leather. I was interested in that, and thought maybe I should learn another trade. If I were to get hurt at the race track, it would come in handy.

When Bobby Isham got to Keeneland, he and Mr. Eddie hit it off right away. We did our jobs, and tried to learn as much as we could. We went home to Lebanon on Saturday afternoon, and came back early Sunday morning so we could get to work on time. We were young, and didn't need much sleep. We were at Keeneland from winter to early spring. I knew we would be going to Churchill Downs in late April. I was thrilled to move to Churchill Downs, but I would miss

Mrs. Rodgers. She was like my mother. I truly loved her. I also would miss going to the leather shop and seeing Paul Ladd, but they would be there when I got back.

At that time, Mr. Eddie had two really good horses. Bumpy Road had just won the Lafayette Stake, and broke the track record. That was a new experience for me, working with a horse that won a stake race.

We won five races at Keeneland, which was good for a small stable. We only had twelve horses. When Mr. Eddie gave us a bonus for Bumpy Road winning, that was another first for us.

We finally got moved to Churchill Downs, and everything we did was a first for us. We were just enjoying life. We run our other good horse, Star Rover, who won at Keeneland and at Churchill, so he was two for two.

Mr. Eddie was thinking about running Bumpy Road in a big stake race in Boston, Massachusetts. One day Mr. Eddie told me and Bobby that we might be taking a train ride. It was very exciting to us to be thinking about riding a train all the way to Boston. We would know all the details in a few days. In the mean time, we kept on working, and talking about our trip.

The day we were supposed to leave, we had to take everything quite a distance to where the train cars were parked. I didn't realize there were three car loads of horses going to Boston. When we got the horses loaded, and was ready to go, Dr. Alex Harthill came over and gave me twenty dollars and told me to make sure his horse had plenty of water on the way up to Boston. He said when the horse run, to take the twenty dollars and bet on him.

When we got to New York, we had a little lay over, so Bobby decided to get off the train and get us something good to eat. He ordered the food, but when he went to pay for it, his wallet was gone. Someone had cut the bottom of his pocket and took his wallet. Someone from another train car gave him some money. He almost missed the train. It was moving when he got on.

We made it to Boston, and when Bumpy Road run, he won. When Dr. Harthill's horse run, we forgot to bet the twenty dollars that he gave us. His horse won and paid sixty dollars to win. I was sick, and for years to come, I paid attention to what Dr. Harthill told me. When we got back from Boston, we stayed at Churchill for the rest of the race meet.

David galloping Bumpy Roads at Keeneland 1958

When Churchill Downs was over we shipped the horses to Garden State Park, in Cherry Hill, New Jersey. Bobby had found a girlfriend, and he decided to stay in Lexington, Kentucky that summer. I didn't know about this "Garden State Park" thing. The first thing I had to do was call my dad and have him send my birth certificate, before I could get a license to work on the race track. Finally I got it all straightened out, and we got on with the job.

Mr. Eddie was such a nice person. He would invite me to their house to eat with them. His wife, Mickie, was nice to me. She would get me to drive her places. I felt very important doing that.

Mr. Eddie was trying to teach me to work horses the right speed. I was learning well, and I got to where I was getting the times pretty close. I didn't get to be around as many blacksmiths as I would have liked, but I thought it would happen eventually. We didn't seem to be there very long, but time flies when you're having fun.

We shipped to Atlantic Park next, and I had been looking forward to going down to the Boardwalk in Atlantic City. It was simply beautiful. The first time I went, I saw the horse jump off the steel pier into the ocean. That was quite a sight.

In a few days Doug Davis shipped in his horse, Burnburgoo, for the biggest turf race they have at Atlantic City Park. The next day Doug asked if I would like to gallop Burnburgoo for him. I said yes. I didn't think I had enough experience to gallop a good horse like him, but everything went well. Before the horse run, Doug had me to blow him out a half mile, and he went perfect. Doug said that now, all we had to do was wait until race day, and W. M. Cook was going to ride him. I really didn't know W. M. Cook, but in later years I got to know him well. Burnburgoo finished third in one of the biggest turf races in the country.

When I saw that W. D. Lucas wasn't' riding Burnburgoo I didn't understand why, since Lucas had ridden him in most of his races, and Burnburgoo had made a lot of money. When I first started working there, W. D. Lucas would pick me up and take me everywhere with him. He was a first class person. I had been very lucky, so far, to meet so many nice people. I had also met Bill Hartack, who rode races for

Mr. Eddie. It was no wonder Mr. Eddie was such a good trainer. He come up under the guidance of Frank Kernes, who trained horses for Calumet farm, before Ben Jones. I couldn't have met better horsemen.

After Garden State Park was coming to a close, I was getting homesick. I had been away from home for several months, and my mother was always writing and telling me to call her. I didn't call much, because that is the way young people are. I told Mr. Eddie that I was going home, and I would try to go back to work for him the first of the year. I headed home in late summer. I went straight to Lebanon.

I saw my mom, and dad, and some of the rest of my family. I hung around with some of the boys I used to be friends with for a few days, and then I went to Keeneland. I saw Al Brumfield, and asked if he knew anyone who needed an exercise boy. He said that he was working for Mac Miller, and he needed someone. Al told me that his brother, Donny Brumfield, was working for Mr. Miller, and that he was going to start riding races. Al said that Mr. Miller was a young trainer who had good horses, and that they were all fillies. He said that one was a super filly, and her name was Leleh. The next morning I met Mr. Miller, and he was a very nice man. He told me I had a job, and if any of the horses was too tough for me to gallop, I should tell him, and he would put a stronger rider on them. I never did have a horse that was too tough for me to gallop. Mr. Eddie told me I would never have any trouble with the horses, because I had good hands.

After I got to Keeneland, I went back to Pinkston's Turf Shop and checked in with Paul Ladd. He said I could hang out there any time I wanted to. I drove out and checked in on Mrs. Rodgers. She said that my room was ready, and nothing had changed. It seemed like you always want to be around good people.

I worked the rest of the summer for Mr. Miller. When the Keeneland meet was over, Mr. Miller said that he would like me to go to Florida with him for the winter. He said he paid his help more money when they were away from home.

While I was working for Mr. Miller, I met a famous blacksmith named Jackie Thompson. He told me the same thing that all the other blacksmiths told me. He said that I should find something else to do besides being a blacksmith. He said that Scoop Sallee was looking for an exercise boy to go with him to New Orleans, and that sounded good to me.

I met Mr. Sallee the next day, and he asked if I could be ready to go with them to the fall meet at Churchill Downs. That sounded great to me.

My Seventeenth birthday was coming up, and I wanted to go home for that. I did get to go, and it was very nice. My mother made me a nice cake, and for the first time I felt funny about starting to become of age.

When it was time to ship the horses, I went to the barn and helped them load everything on to the van. After we got to Churchill Downs, everything had to be unloaded and set up that day. After we were finished I met the other exercise boy. His name was C. L. Martin, but everyone called him Charlie. I didn't know what to think of him. He had already pulled some pranks on me. I could see everyone snickering.

Charlie told me that I could stay with him. He lived on Third Street, just a couple of blocks from the race track. He didn't charge me much rent, because he went home on the week-ends, and was glad to have someone to watch his things.

Charlie was always trying to pull something on somebody. He told me that Mr. Salle was very grumpy, and every time that you asked him something, he would yell at you. I didn't know whether to believe him or not. A few days later, Charlie asked how many times Mr. Sallee had yelled at me. I told him he had been very nice to me. A few days later, he asked me the same question. I told Charlie it was because I was better looking than him, and he didn't bother me any more.

A few days later we were at Charlie's house, and he started telling me a story about when he was riding races. He said he had a bad spill in a race at Churchill Downs, and he was killed. He is telling me this story about being killed, but he looked fine to me. He went on to say that he was taken to the morgue, because they thought that he was dead. A few minutes after they left him there, he woke up, and started walking down one of the halls.

Charlie told me that he was always determined to become a jockey. He started learning to gallop horses at the age of twenty-nine at Calumet farm. Most jockeys are ready to quit riding by that age. Over the next few years, I asked several people about the story he told me, about getting killed, and they would say, "Oh, yes" I remember that accident. He was a very lucky man. It took me a long time to even half way believe it. Just recently I asked on old horseman if he knew the jockey who got killed back in the fifties. He said "yes, sir". That was C. L. Martin. What can you say!

Churchill Downs is a short meet in the fall, and we only won a couple of races. I was wanting to get to New Orleans, since I had heard so much about it. Finally Churchill was over, and Charlie said that he was going to stay home with his family. One of his son-in-laws was a jockey. He was Bobby Deavers.

We shipped the horses the next day. I drove all the way to New Orleans, and got there late at night. That was not good, because I didn't know anyone there. When I found our barn, I had some blankets in my car, so I went upstairs to the tack room and took a nap. The horses didn't get there until after noon. I helped unload everything, and there is a lot of stuff that goes with shipping horses.

While I was there I think it rained every day. Mud was knee deep. One of the first people I met was Fats Domino's brother. He took care of the race track ponies. His barn was right next to ours. I was glad we had gotten there, because I was broke. I knew that we could draw money on our check. The first time I asked Mr. Sallee for twenty dollars, you could have heard him yelling in the next state. I knew then, what Charlie meant, but that was just his way.

I had already made up my mind if I could make it until the last of December, I was going back to Lexington. I knew that Mr. Eddie turned his horses out at the end of the season, and put them back in training on January the first.

I didn't enjoy any of my visit in New Orleans. I could go places, but couldn't do anything legally, because I was only seventeen. If I had been older, it would have been fun, even though the track was muddy and deep. A lot of horses fell while they were galloping in the mornings.

I did enjoy walking over to the centerfield to see Black Gold's grave. He was a super kind of horse. He broke his leg there, and that is why he was buried there. It wouldn't be long before it was time to go home. If I ever came back, I wanted to be old enough to go somewhere and do something.

I decided to leave a week early, so that I could stop in Tennessee and get some fireworks for Christmas. I wanted to go to Papa's house for Christmas. I hadn't seen my grandparents for two years, and I knew they always had a big Christmas every year.

I headed back to Lebanon, Kentucky, and when I got to Tennessee, I stopped at a fireworks store and bought a bushel basket full of fireworks. When I did get home, I had a lot of family to see. I knew that Mr. Eddie wouldn't bring the horses in until after January first, so I didn't have to worry about rushing back to work. I just wanted to have a big Christmas.

My mother always invited all our family to eat at our house on Christmas. There was always enough food to feed an army. I sure did enjoy it all. That night we all went to Papa's house for dinner. After we ate, I went to my car and got the big basket of fireworks that I had bought in Tennessee. All my cousins were there, and even the older folks enjoyed the fireworks. That was a big treat back in those days.

After Christmas I had another week before I had to go back to work. I bought another car. It was a nineteen fifty-two Chevrolet, that seemed to run OK. When the week was over, I knew it was time to go back to Keeneland.

When I got back to Keeneland, the horses were starting to ship in. Mr. Eddie seemed very pleased to see me. I was glad that he wanted me to come back to work. It was slow going, but I was on the right track.

I had visited a couple of small farms at the edge of Lexington the year before, and the farm manager told me that their blacksmith was retiring at the end of the year. He said that they didn't have many horses, but it would be a good place to start trimming a few of them.

In a few days we had all the horses at Keeneland settled in, and Mr. Eddie said that we needed to start galloping a few of them. We only had twelve horses there, but was supposed to get three or four more. That gave me a few horses to gallop, and a few to trim at the farm. It sure made me feel better having a little blacksmith work.

Every day after I finished work, I headed to Pinkston's Turf Shop. Paul was glad to see me, and I was sure glad to be back. Paul actually wanted me to do some work in the shop. He even said that he would pay me for what I did, and that sure sounded good to me.

After we started back training all the horses, everything was running smooth. I was trying to learn everything that I could. At that time, Bobby Isham had a steady girl friend, Nancy, and was working at a place that sold, and serviced, boats. He really wasn't satisfied working there. He asked me to share a room with him on Hanover Street, which was a few houses down from Nancy's house.

We went and looked at the room, and it was nice. The Andersons owned the house, and Mrs. Andersons' father lived there. He was one hundred and six years old. Sometimes when I came home at noon, I would sit and talk to the old gentleman. When his mind was working right, he would tell me about the silver war, and Abraham Lincoln.

I enjoyed living there. Bobby was either working, or at Nancy's house. I went to work early. I got up at four thirty every morning. One morning when I left for work, I saw a huge man leave his driveway on a bicycle. I couldn't imagine anyone riding a bicycle that early in the morning, but later I found out that he was Spec Lacey, the nineteen fifty-six world champion weight lifter, and he was in training.

Later I met his sister, Pat Lacey, who was a few years older than me. She was very nice, and we went out together every once in a while. Much later, I met Ruth Ann Parks, who lived a block from Bobby and me. There was a place up the street called Cramers Corner. They had a jukebox and soda fountain. That is where all the kids in the neighborhood hung out.

Ruth Ann and I went out all that winter until we shipped the horses to Monmouth Park. Bobby was wanting to go back to work for Mr.

Eddie. The winter had passed very fast, and Bobby and I were still going to Lebanon almost every weekend. There is something about home that you just can't explain. When you are young, everything goes through your mind.

When we got to Lebanon, Buford Bradshaw had called my dad and left word for us to come to see him. Buford was getting in bad health, and he wanted to sell his broodmare. I already had one horse, and I didn't need another one. Bobby said that he would like to have her. The mare had been bred to Swing and Sway, which was a nice stud. Buford said that Bobby could have the mare, and he found a place to keep her.

On the way back to Lexington, Bobby said that he was going back to work for Mr. Eddie, as soon as he put the rest of his horses back in training. Bobby wanted to go to Monmouth Park, New Jersey, with us.

It was nice there. The ocean was just a few blocks from the race track. There was a huge amusement park close by, so we should have a nice summer. By this time I had bought a nineteen fifty-six Chevrolet, and it was nice. Keeneland was ready to start, and I knew it wouldn't be long until we would be going there with the horses. Mr. Eddie told us that we had some good two year olds that should win on their first or second start. Two of the horses were Bumpy Roads and Star Rover. They were always tough every time they run. Bobby and I were planning to be gone all summer.

Once Keeneland was over and we got the horses shipped to Monmouth Park, everything was going fine. Bobby and I was enjoying all the new scenery. I went crabbing a few times. Mr. Eddie would invite us to his house, and he would cook the crabs. They were very good to eat.

One day Mr. Eddie gave me a pleasant surprise. He told me he was sending me, and one groom, and four horses to Rockingham Park, in Salem, New Hampshire. In a few days, we were on our way. The groom, Claude Crouch, and the horses rode on the van. I drove my car.

After we got to Rockingham Park, and the horses started running good, Mr. Eddie said that we might stay all summer. I met some very nice people up there. They were different than the people that I was used to being around. We were in the barn with a big stable that had a groom with three daughters. I met them, so I had people to go places with.

I had met a couple of exercise boys that I hung out with, and we had a really good time. They showed me the mountains in Maine. They were very beautiful in the summer, and cool at night. Every day at the race track the temperature was in the high nineties, and very humid, but it seemed like the horses liked it there.

The reason that Mr. Eddie told me I might stay there all summer was because he really trusted me. He knew that I would never lie to him, and would always tell him like it was. We did stay there until September. We left right after my eighteenth birthday. Then we shipped the horses back to Delaware with the rest of our stable. We stayed there until we shipped to Suffolk Downs for the fall meeting.

When we shipped to Suffolk Downs, Bobby Isham said that he was going back to Lexington, because he and his girlfriend, Nancy, were in love. After Bobby left, I managed to meet a few blacksmiths. I was learning slow, but I was also learning a lot about horses in general.

Mr. Eddie couldn't believe how well I was doing. I knew it would be cold when we left Suffolk Downs, and I really didn't like to gallop horses in cold weather, but I had to do what I had to do! While I was there I got to meet Chris McCarron. His agent came by the barn to talk to Mr. Eddie about riding some of our horses. Chris hadn't been riding very long.

If I could have read thirty years into the future, it would have saved me a lot of trouble. Mr. Eddie was getting anxious, because we weren't getting to run very many horses. It was so cold there, I don't know how the horses could run. At night I would sleep in my clothes, put four blankets on my bed, and still be cold. In a few days Mr. Eddie said that he had had enough, and was shipping the horses to Pimlico, Maryland. I sure was glad to get out of Boston.

In two days we were at Pimlico. The weather was good when we shipped in, and the races were good, also. I liked it there. It was right in town, and I could walk anywhere I needed to go. Mr. Eddie said that he had heard the long range weather forecast, and that we were supposed to get a blizzard in less than a week. That was the biggest snow that I had ever seen. You couldn't tell one barn from the other. They closed down all of the Baltimore area, and it was two weeks before we could ship back to Lexington, Kentucky.

When we finally got back home I was sure relieved. I was afraid I would get my car torn up, but we made it OK. Mr. Eddie wanted to turn some of the horses out to give them a little break. This process takes a little time, because you have to turn them loose in a small area a few times, before you can turn them loose in a big paddock. Mr. Eddie said that when we got all the horses turned out, we all had a vacation coming. He said he would pay us for one week, and if we needed two weeks, we could take it. We had been gone for almost a year.

When Mr. Eddie told me we were free to go, I headed to Lebanon, Kentucky. I wanted to see my family, especially my grandfather. He was the reason I got started in this kind of life. I really enjoyed my first vacation. I went to see my three friends that I had always run around with. I also went to see Buford Bradshaw, and he was in good shape.

My vacation started in the middle of the week, and I had done a lot of riding around. On Saturday, I took my car to the shop, and had some glasspack mufflers put on it. (Back in those days, young men who had cars, had to have glasspack mufflers.) After I got my mufflers on, I was riding down the street, and I couldn't believe who I saw. It was Norma Jean Gordon. You can't believe how I felt when I saw her. All those feelings that I had in grade school, were fifty times greater now than they were then.

I waited until later that day when I got home. I got the phone book out. I remembered Norma's parent's name, since they were well known in the community. I looked up her phone number, and dialed the phone. The phone rang, and Norma answered it.

I was so nervous that I could barely say hello. I asked if she knew who I was, and she said "no". I told her it was David Wilson, and she didn't really believe me, because she thought I was dead. I had a cousin who was killed in a hunting accident, and she thought that it was me. When I finally convinced her it was me, you can't believe the feelings I had, just talking to her. If there was ever two people who belong together for life, it was us.

The next few weeks, I think I went out with her almost every day. I knew it was going to be hard for me to go back to work. When I finally got my head on straight, I went back to Lexington. Mr. Eddie still wasn't ready for me to go back to work, so I went to Pinkston's Turf Shop. I had learned a lot about leather, and I enjoyed working there.

One of the men who worked there was teaching me how to do hand tooling on leather. I had already learned how to make ladies purses, and now I was learning to make men's hand tooled wallets. I really wanted to learn how to make holsters and gun belts. I thought I would eventually learn to do that, also.

When I did go back to work with the horses, we had several young, baby, horses. They were less than two years old, and were called yearlings. I decided to stay at the barn in the tack room. They were big rooms, and I didn't need much space. It would be a lot closer to Lebanon from Keeneland, than it was from Lexington. I had planned to go to see Norma three times a week, if everything went well. Norma had a lot to say about that. I just couldn't wait from one day until the next, so I could go back to Lebanon. The more I went, the more I felt like our lives would work out. I guess young people don't think like older people do.

One day Mr. Eddie told me that I needed to get some more sleep. I was on the road too much, and I might have a wreck. Mr. Eddie had gotten some more horses, and he had to hire another exercise boy. His name was James Mahoney, and he was an older guy. Mr. Eddie told me that he would be good at keeping an eye on things. The man wanted to be called Jim, and said that he had trained a lot of horses himself.

Sometimes it is better to work for other trainers, than to train horses yourself.

I can tell you, it was a quick winter. It seemed like I was in Lebanon more than I was at Keeneland. Norma and I seemed to be getting closer to one another. I wanted to be with her all the time, and it wasn't long before I asked her if she would marry me. She said "yes", but I would have to ask her parents.

That weekend I finally got up enough nerve to ask her parents. We were eating in the living room, and I set my plate on the couch. I was so nervous that I sat down in my plate. It was really getting late, and I still hadn't gotten up the nerve to ask if we could get married. Mr. Gordon called Norma into the next room, and told her that he knew what I was going through, and that I didn't have to ask him. I was so relieved. They were such nice people. They were very religious, and very strict. Norma respected her parents very much, and so did I.

We planned to get married on April twenty six. Norma was still in high school, and I knew that I would be leaving with the horses before school was out. I wouldn't get but a couple of days off when we got married, so we were looking for a small apartment in Lebanon. All of this felt very strange.

Norma found a small two room apartment close to where she went to school. When I got there the next week, Norma took me to look at the apartment. It looked fine to me. I was already getting nervous, and our wedding was three weeks away.

Mr. Eddie had moved the horses back to Churchill Downs, and Bobby Isham went back to work as a groom. He had gotten too big to gallop horses, and he and Nancy had already gotten married. Now when I went to Lebanon, I went from Churchill Downs instead of Keeneland. I still hadn't gotten used to moving around so much.

When April 26 rolled around, I worked for a while that morning, and then went to Lebanon. It had been pouring down rain all night, and was still raining that morning. When I got to Norma's, her sister had pulled her car out of the garage, so I could park where it was dry. I was going to dress for the wedding at their house. When we got ready to leave for the church, my car wouldn't start. I was in such a hurry to get there, I had forgotten to put gas in my car. My brother-in-law, Louis, was nice enough to pull their car into the other side of the garage so that we wouldn't get wet.

When we got to the church, we were supposed to have a small wedding, but the whole church was full. Getting married in those days was a big deal. I made it through the wedding, even though I was very nervous. We were married at the First Baptist Church in Lebanon, and our Pastor, Brother Colvin, officiated.

Since it was still pouring down rain. We decided that we would eat dinner at our new home. I loved that idea. I had been running wide open for several months, and it was nice to slow down. When we got to our little apartment, I finally felt like it was real, and fifty-one years later, I know it was.

We were married on Saturday, and I had until Monday to go back to work at Churchill Downs. It was seventy miles to Lebanon, and I would drive it every day. I would be home each day before Norma got out of school. She had one month to go before she graduated from high school. After graduation, our real life would start.

When the Kentucky Derby time came around, I took Norma to Churchill Downs. Bobby went to Lexington and got Nancy, and brought her to the Derby. We all stayed on the backside all day, and didn't think about where we were going to stay that night. There wasn't a room anywhere in Louisville to stay. We had to drive all the way to Bardstown, Kentucky to find a motel room. I thought it was kind of ironic. We stayed in the Wilson Motel.

The next morning we went back to the race track. I had to work for awhile, and it gave Norma a chance to see the horses up close, and to meet everyone. Mr. Eddie was crazy about Norma. She had such a good personality. Every body felt like they had known her forever.

In a few days, Mr. Eddie surprised me. He said that his owner had found a race at Lincoln Downs in Rhode Island. There was a fifty thousand dollar race. Mr. Eddie's owner was Irvin Gushin. I had met Mr. Gushin the year before, when we took Bumpy Road to Boston. That is where he lived.

Mr. Gushin gave me and Bobby a stake from Bumpy Road's winning. Mr. Eddie was surprised, because he said that in all the years he had known Mr. Gushin, he had never given anyone a stake.

When it got closer to the race, Mr. Eddie told me they were thinking about flying Star Rover to Rhode Island instead of vaning him there, and we would be taking the rest of the horses to Delaware. That meant I would be leaving my car at home with Norma. After Star Rover run, we would van him back to Delaware.

When it was time to leave, we had to van Star Rover from Churchill Downs to Keeneland, to catch the plane. I was really leery about flying in a plane with a horse. I hoped they knew what they were doing. My brother brought Norma to Keeneland to pick up my car. When we got ready to load Star Rover, he walked up that ramp like he had done it a hundred times.

It was warm when we left Keeneland, so I only took some summer clothes. When we were ready to take off, I told everyone goodbye, and kissed Norma. That was the first time we had been apart since we were married.

The plane's big engine got loud, and I knew we were getting ready to take off. Everything was going smooth, until the pilot told us we were going to increase our altitude to get up over a storm. When we increased altitude, our ears started popping, and it got very cold. That is when I realized I didn't have any warm clothes.

We flew quite a while before we got over the storm, but it never did get any warmer. When the plane landed, it was snowing, and very cold. No one had told me how cold it was in New England. They put us in a barn, and the tack room had a dirt floor. The groom and I had some horse blankets, but there wasn't any heat in the tack room. I didn't know if I could make it through the night, but once we covered up with the blankets, we were warm.

The next day we got Star Rover ready to go over and run. He really looked sharp. He was a mean horse, and he was snapping and kicking at everything that moved. Mr. Eddie came by the barn to check and see if everything was OK. He said it was time to take him over to run.

He finally settled down when he walked on the track. Star Rover sure looked good. I knew he would run good.

All the horses were in the gate, and the announcer said, "and they are off"! All you could see was Star Rover's white head. He was a gray horse with a lot of white on his head. He lead all the way, until a horse called Paper Tiger come flying by, and beat him by a nose.

The next day the van was there for the horses, so we could head back to Delaware. I sure hoped it was warm when we got back there. I had learned a valuable lesson about weather in New England.

When we got back to Delaware, it was nice. I really liked it there, and it was a nice race track. I called Norma, and it was still two weeks before school was out. I was planning to fly home after her graduation, and bring her to Delaware. Norma got all our things together, and loaded them into our car. I couldn't believe she did all of that. She had even gotten her driver's license.

When I got ready to fly home, Bobby asked if we could pick up his wife, Nancy, and bring her to Delaware with us. I told him we would. I flew back to Lexington and Norma was there to meet me, and we picked up Nancy at her house. We got almost to Delaware, and had a flat tire. I liked to have never got it changed. Everything we had was packed on top of the spare and jack in the trunk of the car. We finally got back on the road, and arrived the next morning in time for me to go to work. It was a very quick trip.

Our first day in Delaware we found an apartment. It was on the fourth floor, but we were young so that didn't matter to us. Our apartment was nearly eight miles from the race track. Since I had been there the year before, I knew all of the fun places to go.

One afternoon I took Norma up in a plane. There was a flying service there that would take two people up at a time. I'm not sure if Norma enjoyed that or not. We also bought her a new swimming suit. Wilmington had a lot of recreational places, and I knew where to go swimming.

The hardest thing I had to do, was get used to living with a mate. I was late for work three or four times the first week, but it all worked out. We enjoyed ourselves every day.

One afternoon, after we run a horse, we had the lead pony out of the stall, and we talked Norma into getting on him. We never dreamed about him taking off, but he did, and it nearly scared Norma to death. We finally got him stopped, and I knew we would never talk her into that again.

After we got used to being married, things were kind of settling down. I knew that I couldn't gallop horses forever. I knew what I really wanted was to be a blacksmith. I knew that I had a lot of horse experience, and there was never a day that I didn't watch every horse that passed by me. I needed to get on with my work. I knew my dream would eventually come true.

While we were there, we met a lot of new people. I met a man named Joe, who told me his wife was very sick, and they didn't know what to do. One of the reasons was because they had two children. One of them was a baby, and the other one was three years old. I knew that was a terrible situation to be in.

A few days after I talked to Joe, I realized I wasn't as satisfied as I should be, and Norma had never said anything, but I knew that she was home sick. I couldn't imagine telling Mr. Eddie that we might leave, but I think my friend Joe had a big influence on my decision to go home. He said his wife was getting worse. The doctors didn't seem to be able to help her, and he didn't know what he was going to do with his kids.

In a few days, I told Mr. Eddie that we were leaving Delaware. Not just to help Joe, but to help Norma and me. I knew if I continued to gallop horses, I would never achieve my goal of being a blacksmith.

When we were ready to leave, Joe asked us if we would take his children to Versailles, Kentucky, to their grandparents. We told him we would be glad to. Norma had a lot of young kids in her family, and she could handle any situation.

We drove all night, and arrived in Versailles at eight o'clock the next morning. The kids were very good. It seemed like they understood what was going on. We found the grandparents house. I went and knocked on the door. The grandfather was waiting for us, and thanked us for being so kind. Norma and I were both raised to help people in need. When we drove away, Norma was crying. I knew she wanted to keep those kids, but couldn't.

I never heard any more from them for several years. I saw Joe at Keeneland Race Track, and he said that his wife had died a few days after we left Delaware. He said that his son was a super athlete, and had earned a full scholarship to college.

After we delivered Joe's kids to their grandparents, we went to Lebanon for a few days. I had been thinking about breaking yearlings at Clairborne Farm, in Paris, Kentucky. It was too early in the year to start that job, so we came back to Lexington to find an apartment. After we were settled I went to check on my friend, Paul Ladd, at the leather shop. The next week I decided to go to Clairborne Farm and check things out.

I already knew who to ask for. Harris Robinson was the head yearling man. He had been with the Handcock family since he was a young boy, in Virginia. Harris was one of the nicest men that I ever met. He called everyone "smack". He told me that they weren't planning on starting with the yearlings for two or three weeks, but since I was there, I could start work the next day. He said we could find something to do. It was unreal how friendly everyone there was.

The next morning Harris told me where to park up by the training barn. When I got there, Harris was already there having coffee. He said, "smack", are you ready to go to work? I said, "yes sir".

He said we had to get a saddle pad, and over girth. Harris was in a Clairborne Farm car, so I got in with him. He took me to a barn that was a long way from where we started. If you didn't know the farm, you would need a road map to find it. Each barn had their own grooms, that stayed there all the time. When we started work, the first thing the groom did was put a shank on the yearling. Then he put a chiftney bit in the yearling's mouth, and turned him a few times in the stall. Then I would go in the stall and put the saddle pad on the yearling's back, and then put the over girth on over the saddle pad. The groom would turn the yearling a few more times in the stall. Some of them were afraid of the over girth, and some of them weren't. I would jump up and down on the horse's back for a few times, and then jump all the way up, and put my leg across the horse's back. Most of them would act pretty good, but some would act really dumb. We went through this process on each yearling.

The first day I got on about thirty yearlings. That was a lot for one person to get on, but I was glad to have a job. Harris told me that was enough for the first day. He said that he would meet me at the training barn every day. I asked him how many yearlings we had to break, and he said about one hundred and thirty.

After about a week, Harris told me to start looking around Lexington for some more exercise boys. He said we would need at least twenty boys. In the weeks to come, Harris talked to me about everything on the farm. He even stopped by the office and introduced me to Mr. Handcock. When I walked out of his office, I felt like I was eight feet tall. The more I worked there, the more I liked it.

In the next few days, I started looking around for more exercise boys. I was in Pinkston's one day, and this famous auctioneer came in the store. Paul told him that I worked at Clairborne Farm, and he said that he had a nephew who wanted to ride horses. I told him I knew where he should go, and who to ask for. He told me his name was Jackie Warner. I was able to find several more boys to go to work.

Everything here was new to me. The first time that I stopped at the office to pick up my check, the lady told me where to go to cash it. She said that the bank was owned by Clairborne Farm. I just couldn't believe where I was working. I knew that I had come a long way from Bradfordsville, Kentucky.

After we got a full crew to work, we were getting on all the horses. I knew a lot about breaking horses, because Buford Bradshaw had given me the Thoroughbred Record magazine when I was thirteen, and I kept up with everything it said to do. When I looked at the name plates on some of the yearlings' halters, it would just about blow my mind to think I was going to get on this horse, and there was no telling how much he would be worth. I really enjoyed working at Clairborne.

Later on when most of the yearlings were galloping good, Arthur Handcock came over from his farm, Stone Place, and told us that he had some yearlings to break. He said that he needed four boys to work for him, after we were finished at Clairborne. I was one of the boys that he picked to work for him.

Every day we would go by Stone Place on our way home from Clairborne. One afternoon I was at Pinkston's, and a gentleman came in to pick up some leather goods for yearling breaking. He asked Paul if he knew any exercise boys. Paul yelled back to me to see if I would be interested in working in the afternoon breaking yearlings. Paul introduced the man to me. He was Jack Concella, Normandy Farm's yearling man. He said that we would start work every day at one o'clock, and that he needed three exercise boys. I knew I could make it work, because I got finished at Stone Place about eleven thirty each day.

I knew that I could find some exercise boys at Clairborne who would be interested. I asked two of the boys the next day, and they agreed to go to work. I was getting on so many horses, that I would dream about them at night.

A few weeks later I went to work, and Jackie Warner was there. They started putting him on horses, and he did well, even though he didn't have very much experience. By now we had eighteen exercise boys. Everything seemed to be running well, to have that many horses.

Once in a while Mr. Handcock would walk up to the track and watch us gallop a few sets of yearlings. If he had company coming with him, they would let us know in advance.

I had gotten to know a few of the boys, and I started hanging around with Johnny Nichols. He broke Bold Ruler, as a yearling, the year before when Clairborne had all those good mares. Now, to see their babies being broke, it is almost unreal.

A lot of the exercise boys that I was working with, turned out to be owners and trainers. Spec Alexander was the starter at Keeneland for a lot of years. I was very fortunate to meet all those people through the years.

One Saturday afternoon I thought I heard a chainsaw coming. I looked up and it was Seth Handcock on a go cart. I had never met Seth, but he was friendly, just like any other young boy.

I was young and alert, and I knew that since Clairborne started breaking yearlings early in the year, they would also quit breaking early in the year. That was OK, because there was a lot of yearling jobs. I was trying to do more trimming and shoeing, but the time just wasn't right yet. I knew it would all work out eventually.

I guess I should feel very lucky. I had married the best girl in the world, and I was healthy. It was scary some times. I would think about what our children might look like. I guess that was normal for young people. One day Norma told me that she was thinking about going to work in a jewelry store. I thought that would be neat. It would give her something to do. It is great to be young and in love, but sometimes it is hard to figure everything out. It usually turned out OK.

Yearling breaking usually lasted for about three months. For years there wasn't enough exercise boys for all the farms to break yearlings at the same time, so that is why some farms broke early, and some broke later.

When the end of the season comes, some of the owners start sending their yearlings to different trainers all over the country, and that was starting to happen. Clairborne Farm was very loyal to their workers. The last one hired, was the first one to be laid off.

We worked for about three more weeks, and Harris Robinson told us that we were going to have a little party up in Paris, Kentucky. He had rented a place, and Clairborne Farm paid for everything. I had never been to a party celebrating the end of the season, before, but it was real nice, and it was for exercise boys only.

I had stopped in Lexington and bought a box of cigarette loads. I loaded a box of cigarettes to pull a joke on the boys at the party. I got the loaded cigarettes mixed up with mine, and when I lit one, it blew up in my face. Everyone got a big laugh out of that. The joke was on me. The party went well, and we all had a good time. Everyone told

Harris how much they enjoyed working with him, and that they would see him next year.

No one knows what is in store for us. Harris passed away later that summer. That was a tremendous shock to Clairborne Farm, and all the hundreds of people who knew him. It was hard to realize that Harris was dead, but we had to go on.

We were still working at Stone Farm and Normandy Farm. They both started late, and it would be November before they would ship their yearlings to Camden, South Carolina.

I found out that Mr. Eddie was going to Florida that year, instead of staying at Keeneland. I had talked to Richard Spiller, who was foreman for Doug Davis, and he said that I could have a job with them whenever I wanted one. Since the farms don't work with the horses on Sunday, we had a little time on the weekend to go to Lebanon and visit our families.

I had talked to my brother, and he said that Charley Montgomery wanted me to call him. I couldn't imagine what he wanted. He was the man who owned Crow Mun, the mare that I rode at the fair when I was younger.

I got in touch with Mr. Montgomery, and he said that he had two, two year old fillies, and he would give me a good deal if I would take them to Keeneland and put them in training. Their names were Society Queen and Society Ann. With me trying to work and train two horses, it would put a big strain on me, but the money sounded good.

Mr. Montgomery told me if I could sell them, I could keep anything over fifteen hundred dollars on Society Ann, and anything over twenty five hundred dollars on Society Queen. I really felt that I could sell them without much problem.

I wasn't very old, but I knew a lot of people. I made arrangements for two stalls at Keeneland. It really worked out well. Clairborne Farm had just quit breaking yearlings, so I had until 10 a.m. before I had to start work at Stone Farm. I had a lot of time to work with the two young horses. I got them cleaned up, and pulled their manes. They really looked good.

I decided to put shoes on them. I had a groom to hold them for me, and I had hardly got started when Jackie Thompson, a good blacksmith, come in the barn. He through a fit because I was working without a blacksmith license. He didn't know that I was part owner of the horses, and it was legal to shoe your own horses without a license.

When he found out I didn't need a license, he apologized, then said he didn't realize that I could already shoe a horse. It actually looked good.

It didn't take long until both horses really looked good, and they were galloping good on the race track. I was hoping to sell both horses before the Keeneland fall race meet started, because I didn't know if I could keep them there during the meet.

It wasn't long before Dr. Reed, from Ohio, came to Keeneland looking for polo ponies. I looked him up, and showed him the two fillies. He liked them both, and asked me about the price.

I told him the price of the horses, and he said that it was too much, but he really liked Society Ann, the cheaper of the two. Dr. Reed told me that he was looking for a little cheaper horses, but that he would keep me in mind.

I kept on working every day getting on yearlings, and one of John Ward's assistant trainers told me that they would need a couple of exercise boys in about three weeks. He said that a lot of their help would be leaving for the winter. They also started later in the mornings, so I could still take care of my fillies. He said that I could work through December, and that seemed to be what I should do.

I knew that Stone Farm would be quitting soon, but I wouldn't have to worry about Normandy Farm for awhile.

A few weeks later, I heard someone call "David". I looked out of the barn, and it was Dr. Reed. He said that he wanted to pick up the filly, Society Ann. He handed me a check, and he had a lead shank in his hand. He put her on a horse trailer, and away they went. I knew that Charley Montgomery would be happy that a veterinarian had bought her.

The next week we went to Springfield, Kentucky to give Mr. Montgomery his check. He pulled his check book out, and wrote me a check for one thousand dollars and thanked me. He said he hoped that I could sell the other filly soon. After we left Springfield we went to Lebanon, and saw some of our family. Then we headed back to Lexington.

In a few days, Stone Farm said that they were getting ready to stop on their yearlings. I was glad, because that was a lot of driving, and Normandy Farm was closer to Lexington.

It wasn't long before I was galloping Society Queen on the race track, and a man came by and asked if she was for sale. I told him she was, and he wanted to know how much I wanted for her. I told him five thousand dollars. I thought I might make a little extra on her. He said he would give me thirty-five hundred in cash, and fifteen hundred on the cuff. I told him that was fine. He said he would give me the fifteen hundred when she won her first race. He was going to Hot Springs, Arkansas, for the winter.

I was young, and trusted everybody. I should have had our deal put in writing, but I didn't. I called Charley and told him what I had done. I would send him the check that the man gave me, and he said that he would send me a check right back, and he did.

I kept up with Society Queen. She won her second start at Hot Springs, but I never did get any more money. I wrote that one up as a learning experience. I knew the extra money would have come in handy, but that is the way life is.

One afternoon when I was working at Normandy Farm, this big car came up to the barn. I asked one of the exercise boys who it was, and he said it was E. Berry Ryan, the boss. I thought he was there to watch his yearling gallop. I guess my yearling boss, Jack, had told him about me, because he didn't go to the other boys, he asked me if I could be at Keeneland the next morning at seven o'clock.

He told me that he had sent a mare down to Keeneland from New York to run in the Spinster Stake, and that Burllio Bieza was flying in early the next morning to work her, and he wanted me to get on the work mare. I told him that it would be an honor to work a horse with Bieza.

The next morning, I was at Keeneland early. Mr. Ryan had gone to the airport to pick up Bieza. When they got back the groom had the horses ready. We got a leg up on the horses, and headed for the race track. When we got on the track, we turned the horses out, to stand. Mr. Ryan told us to jog the horses the wrong way to the half mile pole, then turn around and gallop to the three quarter pole and break off. He wanted me to be about three or four lengths in front of the other mare. He told me to let my mare roll on. The work was going fine, and when we got to the half mile pole, I still had a hand full of horse. I remembered that Mr. Ryan said to let her roll on.

When we got to the sixteenth pole, I could hear the bit rattling in the other mare's mouth, but she never did get up beside us. I was afraid that I would be in trouble, but Mr. Ryan said he guessed that stake mare just didn't work all that well. Mr. Ryan gave me twenty dollars and thanked me, then he took Bieza back to the airport. That sure was a good experience. Those are the things we remember when we think back on our past.

The next day I went to John Ward's farm. It was across the road from Keeneland. I spoke to Buddy Kingsley, and told him that I was ready to go to work. He told me to be there the next morning. It was just a routine job. They broke hundreds of yearlings every year.

Every morning Norma would fix me a large container of coffee to take to work, and while I was out on a horse, someone would borrow most of my coffee. One morning Norma got me a box of Ex-Lax, and I put it in my coffee. It didn't take long to find out who the thief was.

After work every day, I was going by the go cart track. I really wanted to get a go cart. My friend, Jackie Warner, said he would help me with the go cart on Sunday, which was the day that everyone raced their go carts.

There were several Lexington business men who wanted to race go carts, so they bought an abandoned ball park, and turned it in to a race track for go carts. It was really nice. I met Sunny Umstead, who sold go carts. He told me all about the go carts, and I bought one.

Norma had a fit. She said that I would get killed, but Mr. Umstead said that they weren't dangerous, even though I knew they were. It was almost fall, and a perfect time to race go carts.

When we started racing we thought that I had bought a go cart that was a lot faster than the rest of them. I won every race that I ran in. One day they checked my engine size. I had two cycle engines. I mixed castor oil in my gas, and it left an odd smell when the engine was running. It made me feel bad, because it was so easy to win.

One Sunday, one of the other men, whose go cart wasn't finishing very well, asked me to drive his go cart. I was glad to do that, just to see if it made a difference. When they dropped the flag, I was in front, and widened every lap. After I won the race, everyone knew that it wasn't the go cart, it was the driver.

I only weighed one hundred and twenty pounds, and Jackie Warner weighed one hundred and five pounds, so we had a big weight advantage. Some of the other men weighed over two hundred pounds. Racing go carts was the most enjoyable thing that I ever did, but it was also expensive. It made going to work more fun.

I knew after the Keeneland race meet was over, that the yearlings at Normandy Farm would be shipping out and my job at John Ward's would be over at the end of December. I was going to enjoy life just as it was, and then one day, Norma told me she thought she might be pregnant.

I had already talked to Richard Spiller about going to work for Doug Davis. Mr. Davis was a big time trainer. I knew that he liked me, because Doug and Mr. Eddie were the best of friends. Mr. Davis liked to be called Doug. I never felt good about calling him Doug, so I always called him Mr. Davis.

I was supposed to start to work on January second, and I thought that it would be a good job. I would be around some really good blacksmiths. When I did go to work, Mr. Davis was never around. He was always going some place, mostly hunting.

Sometime during the winter, he invited me to come down to High Hope Farm to go goose hunting. I knew they would probably play a trick on me. Doug knew that I had never been goose hunting and they put me in an old out house. It was very small, and there was only one little hole in the back to see through. I thought you were supposed to shoot out of that hole. A couple of geese came over the building, I stuck the big old long goose gun out the hole, and pulled the trigger.

I am surprised that the building didn't fly apart. I couldn't hear for two days. They didn't tell me that I was supposed to step outside before I pulled the trigger. That was a valuable lesson learned. Doug laughed about that for years.

Later on that winter, Doug brought me a solid silver western buckle set. He told me that his father had bought it for thirty five hundred dollars, and he wanted to know if I could make him a hand tooled, white, western belt. I told him that I thought I could. I also told him that it was an honor to do so. I knew it would take a little time to make it, but he said that he was in no hurry.

As the winter went on, he told me one day, that Keeneland would need an outrider during the spring meet, since one of their outriders would be leaving. He asked if I would be interested in the job. I told him yes. I knew that I was years younger than anyone I knew that had been an outrider. I felt very special to be asked to do the job.

I think the longer that Mr. Davis knew me, the better he liked me. I knew that Mr. Davis was a very important man in racing, especially at Keeneland.

One morning Mr. Davis said that he would like to go quail hunting down in Marion County, Kentucky. I had told him it was really good hunting down there, and that I would be glad to go with him. A few days later, he asked if I was ready to go, and I told him I was. I hadn't told anyone where we were going, and I remembered that Mr. Davis accidentally shot Mr. Eddie in the face the year before when they were hunting, but I didn't mention that.

We headed out, and Mr. Davis did all the talking. I was glad of that, because I was really shy about talking to people that I really didn't know.

Mr. Davis was pleased with the bird hunting. I took him to my uncle's farm, and there had always been a lot of quail there. Mr. Davis got his limit in a couple of hours, and we were ready to leave. I was really happy when Mr. Davis put his gun back in the car. On our way back to Lexington, we stopped in Lebanon and ate dinner. I really enjoyed myself.

When the Keeneland race meet finally started, I was very anxious about being an outrider. We had to put our riding clothes on in the jockeys' room. Almost every day I would meet two or three new jockeys. I think the jockeys were always messing with me, because I was so young.

I met little John Adams, and we got to be really good friends for a lot of years. One of the things that I remember most about being an outrider, was the day that a two year old run off the wrong way down the backside of the race track. I finally caught her, but I couldn't stop her. The end of the seven eighth pole was getting close, so I turned the pony cross ways in front of the filly, and got her stopped.

I couldn't believe that the jockey on the filly was Bill Hartack. For months after that, every time I saw him he thanked me again. He knew that I might have saved him from getting hurt.

One of my favorite jockeys was W. D. Lucas. I had met him through Mr. Davis. W. D. rode a lot of horses for Mr. Davis, and he took me everywhere with him. We were always going places together.

I knew that W. D. would go to River Downs to ride for the summer. He was usually leading rider at River Downs, and Mr. Davis was leading trainer. Mr. Davis told me one morning that he had a lot of horses coming in to train, and that most of the two year olds that weren't ready to run, would be shipped to Churchill Downs. I decided that when they went to Churchill, I would drive back and forth each day to work with them.

Norma and I had found a place to live without having to pay rent. All I had to do in return, was to drive the owner of the house, Mr. Clause, to the doctor three times a week for electrical shock treatments. It was a very nice place to live, and I enjoyed the work.

The worst part of working with the horses is that you don't get to stay in one place very long. Even though I was working at Churchill, I could still take Mr. Clause to the doctor. Mr. and Mrs. Clause were fairly healthy, they were just getting older. They didn't trust many people but they trusted Norma and me, because we were honest.

Now that Norma was pregnant, I desperately wanted to get somewhere in my career, that I could do more on my blacksmith training. I kept thinking that some day I would make it.

It seemed like Mr. Davis had horses everywhere, and every time I saw him, he was wearing the white belt that I had made for him. I really enjoyed seeing him wearing his belt.

One of the fillies that was sent to Churchill, was Bell Breeze. I worked her one morning, and I tell you, she could fly. I told the foreman how she had worked, but he said that she wasn't much of a horse. He said that Doug had tried to sell her for thirty-five hundred dollars before she was shipped to Churchill Downs. I didn't say any more, but I knew better.

On Bell Breeze's next work day, I was marked on the board to work her. She worked even better than she had the last time. I knew she could run, but I didn't say any more about her. A few weeks later, Mr. Davis was there. We were walking to the race track with a set of horses, and I told Mr. Davis that he had a stake horse in his midst. He didn't say much.

The next time that Bell Breeze worked, Mr. Davis was there, and he had jockey, Jimmy Nichols, on her. I knew then, that he had listened to me. After the filly worked it was very hush, hush, but I knew that she was a runner.

I didn't ask any more questions, I just kept my ears open. I knew that Mr. John Bell owned her, and that Churchill was going to open in a couple of days. I also knew that they would run her quick. On the second day of racing at Churchill, I look at the overnight, and there was Bell Breeze. I didn't say a word, but on the day she run, I stayed at Churchill instead of going back to Lexington.

I was sitting out by the barn, and I looked up, and there was Mr. Bell. He came over and started talking to me about the filly. I was really surprised that Mr. Davis had already told Mr. Bell about me finding out how fast the filly was. Mr. Bell told me that he was going to bet something for me on the filly. When the race run, it was like a one horse race. She broke in front, and just kept widening.

When Mr. Bell came back to the barn, he handed me a wad of money. I didn't dare count it. I put it in my pocket until Mr. Bell left. He must have bet twenty dollars for me, because I had three hundred, plus, dollars. I didn't realize that Bell Breeze had paid thirty dollars to win. Jimmy Nichols came back to the barn, and gave me another twenty. He said that he didn't realize how good Bell Breeze was. She sure did win easy.

I was spending a lot of time driving from Lexington to Louisville, but I thought that some day I would find the right spot. It wasn't but a few days until Bell Breeze was entered to run again. On race day I stayed to see her run. It was just a rerun of the first race.

Mr. Bell showed up and said that he would bet for me again. When the horses broke out of the gate, Bell Breeze won easier than she did the first race, but she paid fifteen dollars to win this time instead of thirty. I still felt good about telling Mr. Davis that she was a good one. It seemed like we were spending all our time waiting for Bell Breeze to run again, even though Mr. Davis had already won a lot of races at Churchill.

One day Dr. Alex Harthill came by the barn to treat Bell Breeze, and he asked me if I would be interested in a good job. He said that his brother-in-law had a farm in Skylight, Kentucky, and he needed a good man to take care of some Polo ponies. He said that I would probably be able to shoe a few horses after I got to know the neighborhood.

Dr. Harthill said that the man's name was Byron Hilliard, and that I should think about it for a few days. He said that Mr. Hilliard was going to put an ad in the newspaper for help, and there wasn't a big hurry.

In the meantime I found out that Bell Breeze was going to run in the Debutante Stake. I knew that would be a tough race. She was getting a lot of publicity, and I knew she would be a short price. I just hoped that she run good, and safe.

There was a lot going on in my life. Norma told me her due date was June sixth, and that was getting close. On the first of June we decided that she would go to her mother's house, just to be safe. I never knew where I was going to be. When it was Bell Breeze's time to shine, I stayed at Churchill that day, just like the other two races.

Mr. Bell came as usual, and told me the same thing, that he would bet for me. When the race went off, it was a little tougher than the other two, but she still won easily. That made her a lot more valuable. A few days later, Mr. Davis told me that they had sold Bell Breeze to a gentleman in Delaware, for one hundred thousand dollars.

Mr. Davis was second leading trainer at the Churchill meet, and leading trainer at Keeneland. It was a pleasure to be working for him. If I ever get to be a blacksmith, I can say that I sure had a lot of experience.

I would be working at Keeneland now that Churchill Downs meet was over, and I had to focus on my wife, Norma. Her due date had already past. I did have a little free time to think. I had a lot of irons in the fire, just to be nineteen.

Things don't always work out the way they should. The morning I got the call from home, everyone that I worked for knew what was going on. I didn't do anything. I got in my car and drove straight to Lebanon, Kentucky to the hospital. They couldn't believe how quick I got there.

In just a few minutes after I got there, the doctor came out and told us that we had a baby boy, and that everything was fine. I had been telling everyone that my choice of names for the baby was David Wilson, Jr. I wasn't sure what name Norma wanted, but when the time come, she chose David Wilson, Jr., also.

After Norma got back on her feet, we decided to check on the job that Dr. Harthill had told me about. We drove to Churchill Downs and looked up Dr. Harthill. He told me how to get to Byron Hilliard's farm. Dr. Harthill said that he would call Mr. Hilliard and tell him that we were on our way.

When we arrived, Mr. Hilliard introduced himself. He was going to play polo, but he couldn't get the bridle on one of the polo ponies. He asked me if I thought that I might have better luck putting it on than he did. I walked over, picked up the bridle, and put it on.

Mr. Hilliard couldn't believe that I did that so easy. He told me that he had trouble every time he tried to put a bridle on that pony. Later we found out that the pony had bad eyes.

Mr. Hilliard told me what the job consisted of, and I felt like it might be the start of settling down.

Dr. Harthill had told Mr. Hilliard that I knew how to shoe horses, and Mr. Hilliard thought it would be nice for me to have my tools along at the polo games, in case a horse lost a shoe. I knew I had the job if I wanted it.

Mr. Hilliard told us that the house was on the front of the property, where we turned in off Highway 42. I had seen the barn and house as we drove back the lane to the Hilliard's place. The house was a little rough, but livable. We told Mr. Hilliard that we didn't have any furniture, and he said that was alright, because they had a lot of furniture scattered around. He said that they would put enough furniture in the house for us to get by.

I told Mr. Hilliard that we would call him in a couple of days. I wanted Norma to be satisfied. It wasn't any further from home, than Lexington was. On the way home, we decided that it would be a good place for little Davey to play, and for us to live.

The next day I called Mr. Hilliard, and told him that I would take the job. I knew moving wouldn't be easy, since part of our things were in Lebanon, and part of them were in Lexington, and we also had a new baby.

We gave ourselves two weeks to get things together, and when we finally got moved, Mr. Hilliard had put some furniture in the house for us. He also told me he had a gravely mower that I could use to mow our grass.

After we got moved in, things seemed to be OK. I got to meet Mrs. Hilliard, and she was a little different. We had a little gas station, and a little country store, less than a mile up the road.

One day my dad called, and told me he was bringing me a milk cow. I didn't think Norma was going to like that cow! I didn't realize how much I would be gone, and she would have to milk the cow. When we moved from Louisville, the people next door gave us a dog. The dog loved kids, but hated grown people, so Norma felt safe when I had to be gone overnight, with the dog there.

When I got started with the polo ponies, they were easy compared to the race track horses, except for the one with bad eyes. The polo team played at the Harmony Landing Country Club when they weren't playing on the road. Mr. Hilliard told me all the places that we had to go. The best part about going on the road, was that I got paid extra. I could save most of the extra money. I really didn't get paid much compared to what I had made on the race track, but our house and all of the extras were free.

Mr. Hilliard also furnished us two meat hogs, and a large garden that was up by the tobacco patch. All we had to do was plant what we wanted, and his work hands would take care of it for us. When they irrigated the tobacco they would also water the garden, so over all, it was a pretty nice place to live.

Mr. Hilliard told me that he and Mrs. Hilliard would be gone for most of the winter, and that I wouldn't have very much to do. A few days later, he said that they were going to have a party at their house, and that I should clean everything up, and to mow the grass everywhere. The day of the party, I have never seen so many cars. I don't know where they put all of them. The next day Mr. Hilliard called me and asked me to come and help clean up the yard. I couldn't believe what I was finding. There was silver dollars everywhere. I asked Robert, their butler, where all that money come from, and he said that Thurston Morton, a United States Senator, always carried a lot of silver dollars in his pockets. He said that after Thurston had a couple of drinks, he would stand on his head, and that is where the silver dollars come from.

The Hilliards were very influential people, and that is why there were so many people at the party, but they were very good to us. Mr. Hilliard told me that I could use anything in the shop that I wanted to. I even learned to weld there, with his electric welder. I also learned a lot of other things there. Mr. Hilliard had a lot of money, so if I needed something, it didn't make any difference, he would get it for me.

Later on that summer, Dr. Harthill's wife would bring their little girl out to the farm, so she could play with David, Jr. Even though they were small, they really seemed to enjoy playing together. What I really liked about living there, was the sounds at night. There was a lot of Bob cats down around the cliffs by the river, and Mr. Hilliard had a large herd of mixed brama and white faced cattle. There was a lot of different sounds to listen to.

It seemed like we were going somewhere every weekend. When we went to Cincinnati, I was anxious to see if Dr. Reed still had Society Ann. When I got the polo ponies unloaded and tied up, I spotted Dr. Reed's area. I walked over and spoke to him, and he remembered who I was. He was surprised to see me working with polo ponies. He said that Society Ann was one of the best ponies he had, and that she played better than most of the older horses.

One afternoon we were at Harmony Landing Country Club, and I saw Ned Bonnie walking down toward the polo area, on one of the largest horses that I had ever seen. I remembered Smokey Sway, the weanling that Buford Bradshaw raised. Every one had said that he was the largest foal they had ever seen. I knew it just couldn't be him, but when Mr. Bonnie got close enough for me to ask him if that might be Smokey Sway, he said yes, that it was. He wanted to know how I knew the horse, since they didn't call him by that name, and I told him that I had seen the horse as a weanling. Mr. Bonnie could hardly believe me. I felt good about recognizing a horse that I hadn't seen for six years.

Mr. Bonnie told me that Smokey Sway had been a really good jumper. Mr. and Mrs. Bonnie are very good horse people. I had met several very important people that summer. It certainly was a great area to meet people.

Mr. Hilliard had a boat trailer, and he wanted me to build a bed on it, where he could store his gear, when they went to the Bahamas. This was something that I really wanted to do, so that I could use some of my blacksmith skills. I had to do some welding, so that I could bolt the wood on to the trailer.

When I was finished, it really looked good, and Mr. Hilliard was very pleased. He measured the box that I had made, and had a tarp made to fit it. Then I made leather straps to hold the tarp on the box. It was first class. Mr. Hilliard had given me an old army jeep to drive. It would be good for winter. It was about a half mile from the barn to our house.

When Mr. & Mrs. Hilliard went to the Bahamas, I had a two year old horse to break. The horse belonged to Mrs. Hilliard, and seemed to be pretty nice, but when I got on his back, he threw me harder than any other horse that I had ever been on. I couldn't believe it. The worst part was that I was by myself. If I had of had help, it probably wouldn't have happened. I was lucky, and it all worked out OK.

After a few days, the horse started doing fine. I even broke him to lead with one of the polo ponies. After a few weeks he was like an old horse.

It wouldn't be long until cold weather. There was three chainsaws in the shop, and I used one a few times, but I knew they were dangerous. I started cutting wood a couple of times a week, and hauling it to the house in the jeep. I could go anywhere in the jeep. I was starting to like living there. Our milk cow was good to fool with, and when Norma had to milk her, she didn't have any trouble.

I had met Dick Adams, who owned a farm right in the middle of Mr. Hilliard's farm. He was retired, but he still had some cattle to take care of. He knew that we had some meat hogs, and he said that he would be glad to help me kill them. I missed killing hogs, because I had helped my dad every year when I was growing up. There wasn't much to it. I didn't have a scalding box to put the hog in to get the hair off, but Mr. Adams showed me how to scald them without a box. That is why old heads are better than young heads. It all went well, and we had some really nice meat.

I had to take our sausage meat to LaGrange, Kentucky, to get it ground up. Norma had one of our neighbors to make us some sausage sacks, and we knew how to stuff the sausage in the sacks. We had enough food to last forever, without going to the store. We had our own eggs, milk, and fresh meat. Norma had canned pickles that year, and we had a neighbor who loved Norma's pickles, so she would trade a loaf of bread for a jar of pickles.

We tried to get our hogs killed, and canning done before Thanksgiving, so that we could go home and visit our parents. Norma's family always enjoyed Thanksgiving. They also killed hogs, and anything else that they wanted for food. My family had Thanksgiving on a smaller scale, but always had a lot of food. Our oldest child was still little, and not old enough to enjoy my dad's grocery store. We didn't have to rush home, because Mr. Hilliard's farm help would take care of the horses and our cow, while we were gone.

There wasn't much for me to do in the winter time. I did a little hunting, but not much. I mostly hunted when we went home. I would try to out do Norma's brothers but that didn't happen very often. I did hit a bird once, with a bow and arrow, while it was flying trough the air. I don't think I ever shot a bow, again.

In order for me to find something to do, I would help the farm workers. The farm manager, Joe Kemper, would find things that needed to be repaired. I enjoyed fixing things that needed fixing. The shop was a good one, and had every tool that you could imagine.

We had to stop milking our cow, because she was going to have a calf in a few weeks. That would give me even less to do. I met some men who played basketball on the weekend at Liberty school. They invited me to play ball with them, and that gave me a little something to do.

We were looking forward to Christmas. Both of our families always had a big Christmas. One day Norma told me that she thought she might be pregnant again, and that sounded wonderful to me. At least we would have some good news for Christmas.

We had never talked about how many children we might have, but I loved babies. I was always afraid to hold them until they were at least three months old. I guess I thought they might break.

I knew if we could get through Christmas, it wouldn't be long until spring. I hoped I had enough wood cut, because it looked like it was going to be a really cold winter, and we had been snowed in a couple of times, already.

I had Joe Kemper to order me some lumber for the barn. I had several boards to replace. I went to the back of the farm, and cut two big cedar posts to put up a hitching post. I didn't really need it to hitch a horse to, but it was good to set the saddles on to clean them.

When Mr. Hilliard got home from vacation, the told me that he couldn't believe they didn't already have a hitching post. He also told me to make him a list if I needed any blacksmith tools, and he would get them. I did need a few things. He told me if I ever left his farm, that I could keep my tools.

I had done a lot of work around the barn. We had some back doors that wouldn't open, and I got some hinges and fixed them, because the horses enjoyed looking out the open doors. I think Mr. Hilliard liked me so much because I could do anything. I was mostly satisfied on the farm, but I still wondered if I was on the right track. Being nineteen, I felt like I was running out of time. I guess that is how young people think.

It was starting to get spring, and I was getting busy. I was watching the cow, but they don't talk to you like horses do. I would start training the polo ponies, and getting them ready to play polo. Mr. Hilliard had told me last fall, that there was a garden spot down by our house that we could use. He said they would turn the dirt over when it got time.

I already had my garden planned out. I've always put too much stuff in my garden. I feel very fortunate that my parents were good gardeners, and Norma's parents raised a huge garden, so we knew all about raising a garden. Both of us loved flowers, and working in the garden. When you work like I do, if you don't have something to do, you create something.

I was looking forward to starting to play polo again. I always look forward to going to Memphis, Tennessee. I always joke about maybe seeing Elvis, but the most rewarding place I have been was at Chicago last year when we went to Oakbrook. I couldn't believe such a place existed.

All those professional polo players were in the same place. Most of the horses that came there was on a plane. They come from all over the world.

Oldham County polo was a fairly good team. They won about two thirds of their games, but they got much better when they hired Virgil Christian as their leader. Virgil was a good polo player, and a good horseman. I learned a lot from Virgil. He was a cowboy when he was young, and he also worked as a blacksmith in the cavalry. He had a chuckwagon. He would have a couple of parties every year, and he would always have his chuckwagon there. He was a very colorful person.

I had another thing to worry about. Norma was getting closer to her due date, which was sometime in July. She was going to her mother's house before our second baby was born.

At the time all this was going on, our cow had a beautiful baby calf, and was giving a lot of milk. We decided to buy another baby calf to put on her, too, since she was giving about four gallons of milk, after the calf had nursed. Our oldest son, David, Jr., was almost a year old. I guess it is better to have your children while you are young, and grow up with them. I tell you, time sure does fly.

It wouldn't be long until we had the first polo game that we had played for awhile. Mr. Hilliard had gone to Canada for a couple of weeks, to a camp that they owned there. I knew that money was no problem for the Hilliards. They were sure good to Norma and me.

When Mr. Hilliard got back from Canada, he told me that he had bought two new polo ponies. When the ponies got to the farm, there was a message with them. There was a palomino pony, and he was supposed to be good, which he was. It seemed like he could understand what you were saying to him. The other pony was a reddish chestnut, and we were told to be leery of this one, but they didn't say why. After he had been there for a few weeks, he had a loose nail in his shoe, and I was going to fix it. I snapped him to the cross ties, and went to get my blacksmith tools. I put my blacksmith apron on, and bent over to pick up his back foot.

I understood then, why they said to be leery of him. He kicked me so hard that I thought I was going to die. He hit me from the side of my stomach, the foot glancing in my groin area, and I saw stars and everything that goes with them, but I guess I would live.

A few days later, Norma told me that I should probably take her to her mother's house, because she didn't want to wait until the last minute. After I took her home, I had a lot more work to do with the extra horses.

Mr. Hilliard said that he was going to stop using two of the older polo ponies. We only took four ponies to a polo game, mainly because we could only haul four at a time on the horse trailer. Sometimes we would send a pony with someone else, who had room on their trailer.

I had made arrangements with the farm help to take care of everything while we were gone. They were all country boys, and they knew how to take care of the cow and calves.

When I got the call to come home, I went straight to Lebanon. I got there in time to go in the hospital room with Norma. I wasn't all that crazy about being in that room, but it was an experience equal to none. It wasn't long until Dr. Clarkston came out of the delivery room and said I had a big girl.

I was hoping we would have a girl. Norma thought it would be a girl the whole nine months she carried her. I think women kind of know what they are going to have. We named her Tracy Jean. Norma had that name picked out long before she was born. Norma stayed at her mother's for about ten days, and then I went and got her, and brought her home. It was starting to feel like a family.

I knew that I wasn't making enough money to support my family, growing the way it was. Sometimes I wondered if I would ever achieve my goal. I was going to stay positive, and keep working. I felt that when I got a little older, everything would work out.

Norma and I had talked about staying at Hilliard's another year, and she wanted to go to work to help out. I didn't really want her to go to work, but she was going to try it for a while. We had to buy another car, and there would be a baby sitter.

Norma tried working for a while, but it cost more for gas, than what she made. It was a long drive from Goshen to Louisville. Norma finally gave that up, and concentrated on the babies. It was a lovely place to raise kids.

It wouldn't be long until fall. I guessed that Dick Adams would help me kill hogs again, and I really did like cutting wood, but what I liked most was gathering all the fall stuff out of the garden. I was going to tap some maple trees and make some maple syrup. There was a lot of maple trees on Mr. Hilliard's farm.

One day Mr. Hilliard told me that they were planning another big party. I think that was an annual event at their house. I hoped that Thurston Morton would come again with all those silver dollars. I knew when they had a party, my job was to start mowing. I actually liked to mow. I like the smell of cut grass.

After I finished mowing around the barn, I was riding down to my house on the gravely mower. The gravely had a two wheel cart that you could ride on. Where Mr. Hilliard's property ended, and Dick Adam's property started, there was a cattle crossing. I went sailing over the cattle crossing, and when I went over the hump, the pin came out that hooked the gravely and the cart together. The gravely went one way, and the cart went the other way.

It tore all the skin off of my elbows. It was horrible. Luckily, the gravely ran up on some dirt and stopped. I finally got it back together, and went on and mowed my yard. The only thing that it hurt was my feelings, and I lost a little skin. I was looking forward to the big party being over, to see if I could find some more silver dollars. I guess Mr. Hilliard always planned the party near the end of polo season.

Since I have worked for Mr. Hilliard, I have gotten to know a lot of people. One of the people who I got to know, was Warner Jones. Warner owned Hermitage Farm, and the farm manager told me that I should break yearlings for them. He said that he would work it out with Warner and Mr. Hilliard.

A few weeks later, Mr. Jones asked me if I would break yearlings for them, and I told him that I would. This would make my life a little more exciting. Mr. Jones didn't know that I had been breaking yearlings at Clairborne Farm for a couple of years, and I just kept thinking about being a blacksmith.

It is slow going on the farm. All the things that I have dreamed about just don't seem to be taking place. I guess that I was just too anxious. Norma liked the slow, easy, life. The only thing she wanted was to love me and her babies. I was very lucky to find a woman like her.

This past year seems almost identical to last year, except having a new daughter. When they finally did have the big party, I didn't find a single silver dollar. All I found was a lot of garbage. I knew that after the party the Hilliards would go south.

Our oldest son, David, Jr., has been walking for awhile. I had just started to get used to being a father, but it takes some men longer than others. Norma has been canning tomatoes and green beans out of the garden, and I told the farm manager that I would help them cut some tobacco. I used to like to help in the tobacco. I did tap some maple trees, and we got about five gallons of juice from the trees. Norma boiled the juice down, and we got one cup of maple syrup from it. I wrote that one up as good experience.

I really didn't know what was in store for me. I just couldn't read the future. All I had to go on, was my instincts. I guess that I was lucky. I was only twenty years old, and I could shoe a horse pretty well. I just needed to get in a position where I could get some practice. I guess time is the secret to being successful.

I had planned to stay with Mr. Hilliard until next fall. A lot can happen in a year.

When we finally got ready to kill our meat hogs, Mr. Adams wanted to know what we had been feeding them. He couldn't believe how big they were. We finally got through the mess. It takes about a week to work up all the meat. I have always enjoyed killing hogs, and smelling the wood burning under the scalding box. We salted the hams down, and when they cured out, one of them weighed forty-two pounds. That was one of the reasons I enjoyed living there, all that good eating.

I always heard from the older people about time going by so fast. It also goes fast for young people, if you can keep yourself busy. I was looking forward to playing basketball this winter at Liberty school. I dread using wood stoves around the babies, but I guess they will learn to stay away from them. It was extremely cold last winter, but maybe it will be warmer this winter.

I am going to cut some more wood, and I am going to help the farm hands strip tobacco. I don't have to help them, because it's not my job, but it will help pass the time away.

It seems like after Christmas, that spring comes pretty quick. Back in those days, we didn't have television, but we listened to all of the University of Kentucky basketball games on the radio. That was better than television. Some times I would go to sleep with Kentucky several points behind, and only a few seconds to play, and wake up with Kentucky winning the game.

I finally started putting the polo ponies in the barn. I had to clean them up, and they all had to have the hair clipped off that they had grown through the winter. After it got a little warmer, they all had to have shoes put on. The famous Erniest brothers did all the blacksmith work there.

When Mr. Hilliard got home from vacation, he would be pleased, that I had already gotten all of this stuff done. It takes a long time to get all of the saddles and bridles out, and clean them up. Polo ponies require a lot of tack. It takes about a month to get the ponies fit enough to start playing polo. Mrs. Hilliard's horse that I broke last year, was sent to the race track, but he didn't pan out. They said that he was too big, and needed some more time.

After Mr. Hilliard finally got home, we got back into hacking around. They practiced a couple of nights a week, until they got started playing in regular games. One morning I was watching the cow, because she was going to have another calf in April. I went to the house, and Norma was fixing my breakfast. She ran to the bathroom, and I asked her what was wrong. She said she thought she was pregnant again. She said she hadn't had her period for three months. I guess some times women want to be sure before they say anything. Even though that would be three kids really quick, I was tickled to death. I had always loved little babies.

I was glad to get started with the polo games. It would give me a chance to get away some. One of the first games would be in Saint Louis. I had never been there to play polo, since they didn't play there last year. Saint Louis has a lot of history, and I always loved the Budweiser Clydesdales. They are beautiful horses. I had seen them at Churchill Downs.

I was hoping this would be a quick summer. I had already told my dad that he would have to come and get the cow this fall. I don't know where my dad found her, but she was one of the best milk cows I had ever seen.

I run in to Warner Jones at one of the polo games, and he told me not to forget about breaking yearlings for him. We had only been there two years, and I couldn't believe how many people we had met. As the summer moved forward, I was always thinking in the back of my mind, how the easiest way was for me to get on with my blacksmith work. I knew it wasn't going to get any easier, it just takes time.

I worked through the summer, and tried to do a good job. It seemed like everywhere I worked, someone always wanted me to work for them. I knew that said a lot for a person, the way they worked at their job. I always wanted to leave a job with more knowledge than I come with.

I went by Hermitage Farm and met Clay White, who was the yearling man at the farm. I knew him from working in Lexington. He had a big reputation of working with yearlings. I was glad that there was a good horseman there. Things always seem to go better with a smart horseman around.

Clay told me if I wanted to work there, to come to the farm on July the first. He said that Mr. Jones had already talked to him about me. I thanked him, and told him that I would see him then.

We had two more polo games to go to in the next two weeks, and then things slowed down. It would work good for me. I would be done with the yearlings early every day, and then I had the rest of the day to work with the polo ponies. One of our games was in Cincinnati, and the other one was in Columbus, Ohio. They both had good polo teams.

When we were finished with the two polo games, Mr. Hilliard knew that I would probably be leaving. What I didn't know, was that he probably wouldn't play much after this season, because he was getting too old. Playing polo really takes a lot out of you in hot weather. Mr. Hilliard was in his seventies, and the oldest player on the polo team.

On July the first, I reported to work at Hermitage Farm, and Clay White was ready. We started out like all the other good horse farms. We started with the overgirth and pad. The first four days we turned the yearlings both ways in the stall. The horse only has a chifney bit in their mouth. We spent about ten minutes per horse.

After about a week, another exercise boy came to the farm. His name was Jack Fuchs. I had known him from working for Mr. Eddie at Churchill Downs. Jack and I started working two yearlings together out in the shed row. Then two more exercise boys came to the farm. They were Bobby Parrett and Frankie Adams. I knew Bobby from riding in the fairs several years before, and Frankie was still riding a few races. I knew when they came that we had a good crew.

We started taking four yearlings out at a time. We started jogging them around the track a couple of times a day. We did that for a week, and then we started jogging one time around, and galloping one time around, for a week. By then, they were able to go out and gallop every day.

Hermitage Farm horses were like Clairborne Farm horses. They were handled so much as babies, that they were almost broke, when it come time to break them. Once the yearlings get to the point where they gallop every day, it takes some time to soak in before they know what they are doing. They are like children.

One thing happened while I was working at Hermitage, that I will never forget. There was a brood mare that was having trouble having her foal. The farm manager called Dr. Harthill. When he got there, he realized that the foal was dead, and the mare couldn't deliver it normally. He told the farm manager that he would have to cut the foal out of the mare.

When he was finished, he was covered with blood. Dr. Harthill started home, and Warner Jones thought that he would have a little fun. He called the Prospect police, and told them that there was a wild man headed that way, and that he was covered with blood. I never did hear exactly what happened when the Prospect police stopped Dr. Harthill, but I bet Doc invented some new words. People have talked about that for years.

Since we had planned to leave Hilliard's in the fall, we started getting our things together. We didn't have much of our own furniture, so Norma's mother said that we could store whatever we needed to at her house. We planned to make a couple of trips with things later in the summer. I really didn't know what we were going to do, but I knew that something would guide me in the right direction. I knew that I felt really good about breaking yearlings. I guess it was because I knew what I was doing.

The only thing I had to do was exercise the polo ponies in the afternoon, instead of in the morning. When they played polo, it was always on Sunday. We didn't break yearlings on Sunday, so it all worked out well.

I was hoping to be finished at Mr. Hilliard's by the middle of September, so that I could take Norma home to have our third child.

Norma liked to be at her mother's. She didn't have to worry about the other kids, and she knew that someone would be there to get her to the hospital. The baby was due the first part of October. We had been lucky so far. Maybe our luck would hold up.

I was starting to feel old. I would be twenty one the twenty third of September, so I am going to hang in there, and maybe something good will take place. I knew it was seasonal at Hermitage farm, and it certainly was a pleasure working there, but I knew for sure that I would not like to be tied down on a farm all the time.

The farm help told me that Mr. Jones always gave a big bonus at the end of yearling breaking. I had been worried about having enough money to move. Maybe Mr. Hilliard would give me a little extra money, also.

We had really good luck breaking the yearlings. I thought that Mr. Jones would be pleased with our work, and he certainly was. When the work came to an end, he come to the barn and thanked everyone involved, and said to stop by the office, and pick up our checks.

Mr. Jones asked me what I was going to do now, and I told him that I might try to go back to Clairborn Farm for the rest of the season, and go from there. He asked me if I wanted him to call Mr. Hancock for me, since they were good friends. I told him that would tickle me to death. He told me to stop by the farm the next day, and he would tell me what Mr. Hancock said.

I went to the office and picked up my check. It was in an envelope. I waited until I got home to open it, because I wanted Norma to be with me. When we opened it, it almost knocked me over. There was four hundred dollars for my two weeks work, and a five hundred dollar bonus. Back in those days that was a lot of money, so I didn't have to worry so much about moving.

The next morning I went to Mr. Hilliard's, and told him that we were getting things together, so that we could get moved. He gave me my check, and two hundred dollars extra. Since we hadn't gotten any meat hogs that year, he just gave me the extra money. He thanked me for doing such a good job, and said if we were ever back this way to stop in and say hello.

We were going to try to get to Lebanon the next day, so my father was supposed to come and pick up the cow. That was about all that we had left to do. We had already moved just about everything else.

I went by Hermitage farm the next morning, and Mr. Jones said that Mr. Hancock said I had a job whenever I got there. He said that yearling breaking would end at the last of October. He said they had broke two bunches of yearlings that year, and that is why they were still working.

My dad came the next morning to get the cow, and we headed for Lebanon. After Norma and the kids got settled in, I stayed there for a couple of days. I was tired from working two jobs for so long, and then I was headed to Clairborne Farm. When I got there, I met everyone. Some of them I knew, and some I didn't. There was a new yearling man. His name was D. Brooks. He used to be stable agent for Calument farm. I was supposed to start work the next day.

I was very familiar with Clairborne's routine. They walked all the yearlings through a starting gate on their way to the race track, and on their way back from the race track. The third filly I got on, we headed to the track. When we got to the starting gate, I walked her right in, and stopped her. She stood perfect, and I went on to the track and galloped her. When I brought her back, she went in the gate, stopped, and stood perfect, and then walked back to the barn.

When we got to the barn, I took the tack off of her, and they led her away. Mr. Brooks told me that they had tried to get her in the gate all summer, and she wouldn't go in. They couldn't understand why she went in the gate for me. I guess that is why I never had any trouble working places.

The next morning, Mr. Hancock came by the barn and said hello. He told me that he was sure glad I was back working there. I remembered the couple of years that I had worked there. The things that went on was unbelievable. I don't' think there was a bad bred horse on that farm. You could ask who a yearling was, and they would have a mile long list of stakes winners pedigree, on both sides.

One day Mr. Brooks told me that Mr. Hancock was coming to the barn to talk to me about a filly that wasn't acting good. When Mr. Hancock got there, he said that we had to be careful and not hurt this filly, because she was a full sister to Bold Ruler. He said he wanted me to straighten her out, no matter what. I told him that I would try.

The filly was stabled close to the upper part of the race track, and when she would gallop around the track, she wanted to go to her barn. The first time I galloped her, she galloped around the track, and headed for the barn. They told me to carry a whip, that is a no-no on yearlings, and I did.

I used the whip along her nose and shoulder. I didn't want to hit her in the eye. When I got back to the barn and got off her, I told Mr. Brooks that she would probably quit doing that if they would change her barn. Mr. Brooks said that he would ask Mr. Hancock if they could do that, and Mr. Hancock said to do whatever I thought would work. They changed her barn, it worked, and I never had any more trouble with her. I knew Mr. Hancock trusted my decision. He remembered when I was working there before.

We got a yearling in from the Saratoga's sale. At that time, he was the highest priced yearling to ever sell at Saratoga. I think he sold for eighty six thousand dollars, and when he got to Clairborne Farm, Mr. Hancock told the yearling manager not to let anyone else get on this yearling but me. You can't imagine how I felt when he told me what Mr. Hancock had said. I think my hat size got a lot bigger.

One time the exercise boys wanted more money for gas, since they were driving all the way to Paris, Kentucky to work. They all elected me to be the spokesperson, so I went to Mr. Hancock's office. I told him that I had been elected to bring him this message. I said that the exercise boys wanted more money to work. Mr. Hancock told me that the owners would only pay a certain amount to get their horses broke, and if they didn't want to work for what they were getting paid, he would send the yearlings somewhere else to get them broke, since Clairborne didn't make very much for breaking them. Mr. Hancock told me that he respected me for coming to talk to him, and that I was the only one who would get a raise.

There were times when I thought about giving up the idea of being a blacksmith, especially right now. I knew in my heart that I could stay at Clairborne Farm for the rest of my life, if I wanted to. I was just twenty one, and I knew how to shoe a horse, I just needed practice.

When I got home that day, I got a call. Norma was in the hospital, so I went to Lebanon. It took a little longer this time than with the other two babies, but later that day, we had another little girl. I called Clairborne Farm, and asked for the next day off. Norma had already picked out a name, and Tammy Jo Wilson sounded good to me.

I was anxious to get back to work. I stopped and got a box of cigars to give out to the guys at work. When I got there, I felt a lot taller than I did the day before. I really felt good. Having a family was a wonderful feeling. I was hoping to learn what I might be doing with my life. Having three kids meant that I would have to bear down, but I still felt confident. So far I had been a very lucky person.

I kept on working, but I would go home a couple of times a week. As small as they were, our children really loved Norma's parents. Her mother loved everyone, and her father was a quiet man, but he loved his family.

I was working one morning when Mr. Hancock came up to the training barn, and asked me how I would like to go to Florida for the winter. He said that I needed to work for someone like Mr. Fitzsimmons. He said that he had talked to him, and Mr. Fitz said that he would give me a job whenever I got there. Mr. Hancock said that he would pay all my expenses to Florida. He went on to say that Moody Jolley, who was Clairborne Farm's trainer, would be stabled next to Mr. Fitzsimmons. He said that maybe I could keep an eye on his horses.

I never knew why Mr. Hancock liked me so much. I always thought he had big plans for me, later on, when I got a little older. Mr. Hancock was one of the smartest horsemen that I, and a lot of other people, ever knew. I told him that I would have to talk to my wife. Our baby, and the other kids, was awfully young, and Florida was a long way from home. It would have to be Norma's decision.

Norma was young, and I wasn't sure if she could look as far ahead as I could, but I still trusted her decision. When I got to Lebanon we talked it over, and she said if I wanted to go, that it would be OK with her. I knew that this was the biggest move that I had ever made, toward meeting some very important people.

There wasn't anyone in racing more important than Sunny Jim Fitzsimmons, and I felt very honored to work for a legend. I was so excited that I could hardly do my work, but I did go by Pinkston's Turf Shop, and talk to Paul Ladd a few times before we left Lexington.

I knew that it would be two or three weeks before we could make the move. It would give me time to get everything ready, and the baby would be a little older. I kept right on working, trying to get everything together. We still had a few things in Lexington, and in Lebanon, that we had to pick up.

I knew that it would be different working for Mr. Fitz. All of his help had been with him for years. Some of the grooms only worked in the winter. They were semi retired. One of the men that worked for Clairborne Farms used to work for Mr. Fitz, and he was giving me this information. I knew that he knew what he was talking about.

When we were finally ready to leave Lexington, I stopped by the office at Clairborne Farm, and picked up my check and expense money. I told Mr. Hancock how much I appreciated him helping us, and we headed out. I drove at a moderate speed, because the car was loaded heavy. There wasn't enough room left in the trunk for a toothpick. I hoped we didn't have any trouble.

I drove all day, and we didn't get a motel, but we stopped often, and there was a lot of places to lounge around and get a little rest. We were doing fine, until early the next morning. I heard a "pop", and knew it was exactly what I dreaded the most, a flat tire. We were lucky, because it was early in the morning, and the traffic wasn't that heavy, yet. I had to take everything out of the trunk of the car and lay it on the side of the road. Then I changed the tire and put everything back where it was. It took about an hour to do all this.

We didn't have to be in any hurry, so we headed on toward South Florida. When we finally got there, I pulled inside the gate at Hialeah Race Track. I knew which barn that Mr. Fitz was in, so I found it easily. I went in the barn and asked who the foreman was. The man I was talking to said that he was the foreman, and his name was Jasper.

I didn't know about this guy, but after we talked a little bit, I realized that he just had that foreman attitude. I told him that Mr. Hancock had sent me down from the farm, and he said wait just a minute. He went over and talked to Mr. Fitz, and in a minute he yelled my name. He told me to come over to where they were standing, and he introduced me to Mr. Fitz.

Mr. Fitz asked me to sit down with him for awhile, so that we could talk. He asked me some questions, and said that Mr. Hancock had called him and talked to him about me. He said that I had come highly recommended. He said to ask Jasper what he had in mind for me to do.

Jasper told me that there was some houses for rent, just out the back gate. We drove down the street about a half block from the track, and there was two houses for rent. We went in the first house, and looked around. I thought it would be nice to be able to walk to work. The rent was reasonable, and we even had two orange trees in the back yard.

The best part was, that we could pay our rent by the month, without signing a lease. We rented the house, and it was furnished with enough furniture that we could get by. After we had lived there for a few days, we realized why the rent was so cheap. The house was infested with fleas, bugs, and ants by the millions. I told Norma that we would stay there for one month, and that would give us time to find something that we felt good about living in.

The next morning, I reported to work. Jasper gave me a pencil, and told me to take all the two year olds temperature. There was a temperature card on all the stall doors to write the temperatures on, and that was my job for the first week.

One day Jasper told me if I needed money through the week, there was a basket hanging at the end of the barn with a pad and pencil in it. All you had to do was write your name, and how much money you needed. When training hours were over, Mr. Fitz's son, John, was the secretary, and he would put your check in the basket. That was nice to know, in case we needed milk or something during the week.

After a week of taking temperatures every morning, Mr. Fitz wanted me to sit with him when the yearlings went to the race track every morning, and tell him who they were. I was the only one there who knew their names. It seemed like I had a super job, but I knew that it wouldn't last, because we had twenty horses at Hialeah, and forty at Tropical Park.

Everything seemed to be going fine, until we got a new three year old filly in the barn. The groom told me that he would give me five dollars to hold her for the blacksmith when he come to shoe her. I told him that I would be happy to hold the filly, since I wanted to meet the blacksmith any way. I knew that he had to be a good blacksmith to be working for Mr. Fitz.

In a couple of days, the blacksmith showed up, and the groom told him that I was going to hold the filly for him. I had a chance to talk to the blacksmith, his nick name was Nick. I told him that I had been shoeing horses for a long time, but I didn't think I had enough experience to work at the race track yet. I was hoping that he might give me some pointers.

He told me that he would give me all the help he could. I also found out that he worked for Mr. Fitz at Belmont Park. That would give me a long time to find out more about blacksmithing. The groom couldn't figure out why the filly was standing so good for me. I found out that her name was Auction Block, and the more I heard that name, the more I found out about her.

Two days later, my name was on the exercise board, to walk Auction Block under tack. I thought that maybe I as going to get to ride her. When I first got on her, she danced around and jumped up and down, a little. I talked to her, and she settled right down. She was so small, that she looked like a quarter horse, and felt just as quick.

We walked her under tack all that week, and Monday morning she was down on the board to gallop. When she started out of the barn, the pony boy took hold of her bridle. I didn't like that idea. She just about tore the race track down. Come to find out, she couldn't be galloped as a two year old.

When we got back to the barn I told Mr. Fitz if he would let me get a snake bit, and get the pony away from her, that I could gallop her. He said "sonny" you can't gallop her. I didn't say any more, but the next morning he sent his son, John, to the tack store to get me a snake bit. They didn't say a word to me when they led her out of the stall. I went to get on her, and before I saw the snake bit, Mr. Fitz told the pony boy not to take hold of her. I think he wanted to show me that I couldn't gallop her. When we jogged off, she wanted to take off like she did as a two year old, but I kept talking to her, and she settled right down.

I knew that I had earned a feather in my cap. When I got back to the barn, I found out that several people had been watching her on the race track, and I didn't even know that they were watching. Mr. Fitz told me that he really didn't think that I could gallop her. I told Mr. Fitz that she would get easy to gallop, because she listened when you talked to her. Mr. Fitz told me that she would be a really nice mare, if I could handle her, and I told him that I thought I could. I had been on a lot of tough horses, and I never forgot what Mr. Eddie told me. He said that I really had good hands on a horse.

After taking temperatures every morning, I started getting on Auction Block. A few days later, Jasper told me that he was going to assign me two more two years olds to get on every day. One was Highness, and the other was Bold Commander. They were both super bred horses. Highness was a full sister to Bold Ruler. She was the yearling that I had straightened out at the farm. Now, I found out that she had another bad habit. When you were walking her back from the race track, she would drop down on her knees and roll in the sand. She didn't care about me or the saddle being on her back. It just about scared me to death the first time she did that while I was on her. You really had to pay attention to keep her from doing that.

Then one morning we had some more excitement. We were galloping six two year olds, two abreast across the track, when a horse breezed by us. Just as the horse worked by us, he fell dead in the middle of the race track. The two year olds that we were galloping went in every direction, and every rider came off except me. The only reason I didn't fall off was because I was on Bold Commander, and he was so big, and slow thinking, that it didn't scare him. I knew he would be a good horse, but most big horses take longer to mature.

I was getting to know all the help at the barn. There was three or four grooms that wanted to take the afternoon off. They didn't have anyone that they could trust to take care of their horses, so they started asking me if I would help them. I told them that I would be happy to help out. They knew that I needed extra money, so they would give me fifteen dollars every time I worked for them. I could only take care of two people's horses at a time. Jasper had told them it was OK for me to help them.

By now they all knew that Mr. Fitz really liked me. There was actually a little jealousy, since all of Mr. Fitz's help had been there for a long time, and I was a complete stranger. Chico was Mr. Fitz's pony boy, and he liked me, and told me things that I should and shouldn't do. He was a good man.

After I had worked there for a while, one of the older grooms asked if my wife and kids would like to go to the beach. He said that he would pay for everything if we would take him and his wife with us. I told him that I would ask my wife, and be back in a few minutes. Norma said that she would love to go, so we went to the beach that day, and had a really good time. Our two oldest kids loved to play in the sand, but we had to be a little more careful with the baby.

As the days went by, we started a fad. The grooms would ask if I was working for anyone that afternoon, and if I wasn't, they would ask if we wanted to go to the beach. We actually went to the beach all winter, and it was usually free, because the grooms would pay everything, if we would take them with us. We didn't mind, because we really enjoyed the beach.

I had gotten to know my way around the barn area pretty well. One day I walked over to Moody Jolly's barn, and I knew a few of the guys that was working for him. Leroy Jolly was just a young boy at the time. They were stabled on one side of our barn, and Crimson King Farm was stabled on the other side. Crimson King had a derby horse in their stable, and his name was Crimson Saten. Since we were stabled by a derby horse, we always had a lot of action going on around us.

One day, as we were going to the beach, we passed a mobile home park with mobile homes for rent. I stopped and checked it out, and it really did look good. It was back off the street, and the rent was less than what we were paying for the house. It was on seventy ninth street, which was half way between the race track and the beach. When I finished work the next day, I picked up Norma and the kids, and we went and looked at the place. We liked it, so we rented it. Everything was furnished, so it didn't take us long to move. The best part was that we didn't see any bugs. The back yard was shady in the afternoon, so the kids could play outside. We all liked living there.

The early part of the winter was pretty much routine. I worked in the afternoon every day that I could, so that I could make some extra money. Nick, the blacksmith, was there almost every day. It was always a pleasure to talk to him. He was the only one who encouraged me to be a blacksmith. He said that I was going about it the right way, by learning a little more all the time.

Norma turned twenty one on December the ninth. A little while after her birthday, we had company from Kentucky. Her sister and family came to see us for a few days. It sure was good to see her family.

One day while we were driving down seventy ninth street, we saw a night club called the Tropicana Bar. They were advertising country music on the weekends. I knew that Norma was a really good singer, so I told her since she was twenty one now, that we should go over some weekend and she could sing. That didn't go over very well with her, because she had never been in a bar. I kept on talking to her about singing, and I stopped at the bar a few times after work. I told the people who owned the bar that my wife was a really good singer, but she didn't like to go places that sold alcohol.

After I begged her for a couple of weeks, she finally agreed to go. We had to get a baby sitter, but we went. After we were there for a little while, one of the guys from the band came over and introduced himself, and got some information about Norma. When they introduced her to come up on stage, Norma acted like she had done that a hundred times. She sang two songs each hour, and the people couldn't believe she could walk in off the street and sing that good. I knew more than they did.

One week when Norma went over to sing, a man told us about a club called the Peppermint Lounge. We actually went there a few times, and there was a lot of twisting going on. Not long before we were to leave Florida, there was a nationwide twist contest at the Miami Beach Auditorium. The day it started, we were there, and you can't believer how many hundreds of couples that were there. The contest started about noon, and the last couple standing was the winner. We twisted until the next morning, and I had to quit and go to work. When we left, it didn't look like anyone else had quit. I can't believe we did that, but that is why they say young people are crazy.

Now I had to concentrate on my work. All the other horses were going good on the track, and Auction Block was galloping nice. I had secured my job forever by being able to gallop her. On Saturday, Hitting Away won a one hundred thousand dollar added race at Hileah, but most of the older horses were stabled at Tropical Park. The two year olds were broke so good, that when they got to Hileah, they acted like old horses. The owners who have the big money, can get more done with their horses. I guess it will always be that way.

Mr. Fitz was worried that I wouldn't go to New York. I don't think any of his other exercise boys would try to gallop Auction Block, because they were all scared of her. Last year I promised Mr. Fitz that I would stay at Belmont Park until Auction Block run, and then I was going home to be with my family.

I would never be able to live in New York permanently. I went down town a couple of times with one of my friends. While we were on fifty second street, a gentleman gave us some tickets for the Johnny Carson show. I had never heard of him, but come to find out, that was the start of the Johnny Carson show. They were in New York for a few months, and then they moved the show to California. I have talked about that experience for the rest of my life.

Mr. Fitz had already told me if I would go to New York, that he would pay for taking my family home, and flying me to New York. Everything was getting in place, and I had heard Mr. Fitz order the train cars that would be taking the horses from Florida to New York. It takes a lot of work to manage sixty horses.

I called Mr. Eddie, who was at Gulf Stream Park, and talked to him for a while. I told him that I was going to stop by and see him on my way home. A few days before we were going to leave, Norma started getting sick. She really didn't tell me what was wrong, but I decided not to stop and see Mr. Eddie. Instead, we just headed on home to Kentucky. Norma didn't say much, but I had to stop several times during the night, and I was trying to get home as soon as possible.

The next morning, Norma looked over at me and said that she thought she was going to die, and then fell over in the car seat. Now I was driving with three little kids, by myself, I nearly went crazy. We were just outside of Summerset, Kentucky, and I couldn't find the hospital. By then, Norma had come to, and told me to try to get home and not wreck the car.

I don't know how I made it on to Lebanon, but when I got to my mother's house, I stopped, and she come out to the car. She could see that something was wrong, so she took the kids out of the car, and I took Norma to the Lebanon Hospital. When I got her in the building, I thought that I was going to have a heart attack.

They had already taken Norma back to the emergency room, and I had to go to the office and fill out the paper work. I started trying to write, and I couldn't even spell my own name. I told the lady in the office that I needed to sit down and get myself together, and she said

OK. I sat down, put my head on the chair, and just rested for a few minutes. I had been going through this for twenty-four hours. I finally got myself together and filled the paper work out.

In a little while, the doctor came out of the emergency room, and told me that Norma had had a miscarriage, and had lost a lot of blood. He said that she was very weak, and it would take two or three days for her to get strong enough to move around. I hadn't even thought about going to New York. I probably couldn't get in touch with anyone, since they were all moving, too.

I wasn't going to do anything until I knew that Norma was safe. I waited two more days, and then decided to call Belmont Park. I got in touch with John, the foreman, and told him what had happened to Norma. Mr. Fitz had already told John that they weren't going to send Auction Block to the track until I got there. I told John that my brother was going to take me to the Louisville, Kentucky airport the next morning to catch a plane.

John told me to do whatever I had to do to get there. I knew there wouldn't be any problem. The next morning, my brother, Billy, took me to the airport. I got on a flight to New York. I told Billy that I would see him in a few weeks.

When we got to New York, it was late afternoon. There was so much fog that they couldn't land at Idlewild airport, so they started a circling pattern. The pilot told us that they were going to burn some fuel, and try to land in Newark, New Jersey, with radar. I had never been so scared before in my life. There was a man sitting in the seat beside me that worked for the airline. If it hadn't been for him I don't know if I could have made it. He said it was routine to burn fuel in certain cases. I still didn't like it, but he kept me settled down.

When I knew we were going in to land, I tightened up. I felt the wheels hit the runway, and I didn't hear an explosion, so I thought that I might make it after all. I relaxed a little, but now I had another big problem. I was still a long way from Belmont Park.

The airline put me on a bus into New York, and then I got on the subway to get to Long Island. I had a hundred pound trunk with all my belongings in it. This took me all night. Someone told me where to get off the subway, and then I had to catch a cab to take me to the race track. When I walked through the gate at Belmont Park, the guard called John, and he came down and picked me up. He showed me the house where we would be living, and told me to get some rest, that he would see me the next morning at work.

The next morning when I walked in the barn to go to work, not a word was said, even though I was a week late getting there. The first horse I got on to gallop, was Auction Block. Jasper said that I had a new filly to get on, and that her name was Broadway. He said that my three regular horses to get on, was Broadway, Bold Commander, and Auction Block. (At the end of Broadway's life, she was one of the best over all mares to ever live.) I reassured Mr. Fitz that I wouldn't leave New York until Auction Block was ready to run.

I was making some plans, so that when I was ready to leave New York, I wouldn't have that much to do. I really felt bad about leaving Mr. Fitz, but I knew at some point that I needed to get back to my family. Almost every morning, John would come over and ask me to eat with him and his dad. Mr. Fitz had a house next door to where we lived. I knew the other exercise boys were jealous. I just thought it was an honor to be working for such a legend.

Every day, I walked up and down the streets looking for a car that I might be able to buy. I didn't realize that cars were so cheap in New York, but the insurance was extremely high. I found a forty nine Cadillac that was in mint condition, and when I asked the price of the car, I found out that it was only one hundred dollars. Then I found out that the insurance would be almost two thousand dollars.

I asked the salesman if I could buy the car and send the bill of sales to Lebanon and get them changed in Kentucky. He said yes, so I bought the car and sent the papers to Norma, in Lebanon, Kentucky. She had the bill of sales changed, put some liability insurance on the car, and sent me the new license plate and papers. I received everything in a couple of days, and took them to the car lot and picked up my car. I couldn't believe how nice it was. Now I had a way to get around, because Belmont Park is larger than a city. I needed a big car, because I had a big television, and it would fit in the trunk of the car. They had shipped the television to New York on the train with the horses.

I had been in New York for two months, and one day I got a letter from Norma telling me to come home, or else. I knew the Lord was watching out for me, because two days later I saw Auction Block's name on the overnight. When I saw that, I knew that she was ready to run. I walked over to the barn that afternoon, and Jasper told me that I wouldn't have to gallop Auction Block the next morning, because Headley Woodhouse was coming to work her out of the gate.

The next morning, Headley come to the barn in his big Cadillac. He wanted me to get on Auction Block and take her to the gate. Then he would get on her and work her out of the gate, and I could drive his car back to the barn. I knew that was the last time I would ever get on Auction Block, but I did watch her work, and she was simply flying.

When we finished work that day, it was Saturday, and I got paid. I packed my things, and got one of the exercise boys to help me put my television in the trunk of the car. Then I sat down and wrote John Fitzsimmons a long letter explaining why I needed to go home. I told him how much I admired his father. I knew that he was getting very old, and that job wouldn't last forever. Mr. Fitz had raised an army of people in his lifetime. I thanked him, and gave the letter to the boy who had helped me put the television in the car. He said he would give the letter to John. I got in my car and drove down to New York and went through the Holland Tunnel. I was afraid that it might fall in on me, but I made it through. That was in June, Nineteen Sixty Two, and I haven't been back to New York since then.

When I got to the Jersey turnpike, I decided to go through West Virginia. I thought the mountains were beautiful, and I would be able to drive slower and enjoy my Cadillac. I needed to do a lot of thinking. I was still young, and I shouldn't be in a hurry. I also knew that every job I took wouldn't pay enough money to do the things I needed to do for my family. That is why I wanted to be a blacksmith. I knew that they made good money. As I headed on to Lebanon, Kentucky, I knew that I was going to have to take one of those jobs, and just thank God that I was a good exercise boy.

When I finally got to Lexington, Kentucky, I went out to Keeneland Race Track. The only person that I saw was Buddy Kingsley. He told me that they were getting ready to start breaking some yearlings in about a week. I told him that I would be back and check with him. Buddy worked for John Ward, and I had worked there last fall, breaking yearlings. I felt better about talking to Buddy before I got home. At least I would have something for us to look forward to when I got there. I wasn't going to go anywhere for a couple of days. I was tired of running up and down the roads. When I finally got home, my babies looked like they were half grown, and Norma looked good after going through her ordeal.

After I was home for a couple of days, we started talking about what we were going to do. I told Norma what I had found out about going to work, and we decided to go to Lexington over the weekend and look for a house, while we had her family to watch the kids. We found a little house just a few blocks from downtown, and not too far from Keeneland. I could drive to Pinkston's Turf Shop, and Keeneland both, in just a few minutes. It would be easy to move, because we didn't have very much furniture. After we rented the house, we drove back home. I knew Norma's family didn't want us to move back to Lexington, but you have to do what you have to do.

On our moving day, we had no problems, but we had two cars to move in. My Cadillac was as big as a truck, so we had plenty of room. When we got settled in, I went to Keeneland and checked in with Buddy. He told me to come to work when ever I was ready. I told him that I would be there the next day. I went to Pinkston's, and Paul told me that I could work there for him every afternoon. I guessed that would be my life for a while, breaking yearlings and working in the leather shop. I really liked working with the leather, because I could make so many different things.

Over a period of time, I became very good at putting new trees in exercise saddles. When someone brought a saddle in the store, Paul would lay it on my work bench. No one else wanted to fool with putting the tree in a saddle. There was a lot of things that I did well, and if I couldn't, it didn't take long to learn. I worked with the horses until cold weather, and Paul kept asking me to go to work for him full time. I kept thinking about my blacksmith work. I knew I wouldn't make enough money to keep things going, but Paul let me make extra money, so we talked it over. At least I would be working in the warm all winter. After I started working full time, everything was good except how much money that I was making. Then Paul started wanting me to buy a house.

I guess that I was too young to see straight. I didn't know what I was getting in to. While I was working, I did meet some very important people. John Lair used to come in the store regularly. He owned Renfro Valley, and he also owned hackney ponies. There was another time that Step and Fetchet, the black gentleman who played in the Shirley Temple movies, came in the store. He was some kind of a funny man. He came in to get some leather straps made.

As things progressed, Paul found us a house. We went and looked at it, and it was a nice little house, in a good neighborhood. The price was right, and Paul said that Mr. Pinkston would finance the house for us. I knew that I wasn't doing the right thing, and that I was getting in a bind.

We bought the house, and got moved in. We didn't have much, but family gave us a few pieces of furniture. We bought some things, and was doing fine, except there wasn't ever enough money. During the winter I started working part time at a filling station, but it was hard to work two jobs and do them right. By the next spring, Norma decided to go to work and help out. She got a job at Square D. and went to work, but then she had to have a baby sitter. That created more problems than it solved.

We worked like that for another year. I got a weeks vacation in late summer, and we would go fishing, and frog gigging, and trying to do all the normal things. Everything about our lives, Paul was in control of. Paul worked in the ticket office at University of Kentucky, and he would give us tickets to the games, if he felt like it. I felt like everything I did was a waste of time. I felt like people didn't trust what I was doing, and I didn't know what to do about it. The more I worked, the worse it got.

Later on that summer, Norma quit work, and said that she was going to move back to Lebanon, Kentucky. I called my brother-in-law, and he brought his truck, and moved us to Lebanon. We found a little apartment for the time being, and I didn't go back to work for a few days.

On Saturday morning, Paul knocked on the door, and I let him in. Paul wanted to know what I was going to do. I told him that I didn't know. I didn't know what direction to turn, but I told him that I would be back to work on Monday. I told him that I was going to rent the house out for awhile, until we could work things out. I did go to work on Monday, but things were never the same. Paul was upset, because we had broke out of the hold that he had on us. For several days, all I could hear was my father's words. That I would never amount to a hill of beans. I could not let that happen. I was determined to go through with my life's dream. I was not going to give up.

I started driving to Lexington every day, but after a while it became too expensive. One day I stopped by to see the people who I used to take to the doctor. Mrs. Clause came to the door, and I talked to her for a while. She said that Mr. Clause was doing fine. I asked her if I could stay there for a little while, and I explained the reason I wanted to stay. She told me that I knew where the apartment was, and that she might ask me to help her some, for the rent. That would be all it would cost me.

I tried to drive home as much as I could, but after a few weeks of that, I think fate played a big part in my life. The brakes went out on my car, and I had no way to go anywhere. Then the people who had rented our house called and said that the septic tank was backing up in the house, and the plumber told them it would have to have a whole new system. That was too expensive for us, so I called Paul and told him to take the house. I called Norma, and she got my brother-in-law to come and help me get the car home. It didn't take much to fix the brakes. Paul knew that I probably wouldn't be back. After a few days, I went to work for a friend who owned a gas station.

I didn't know how long I might work at the gas station. The owner was almost family, so it would be up to me. I felt good about moving back to Lebanon. My good friend, Bobby Isham, had gotten a divorce, and also moved back to Lebanon. After Bobby moved back, he met a local girl. They got married, and had two children. Bobby and I saw each other quite often.

One day Bobby and I found out that Buford Bradshaw was very sick. In just a few days, Buford died. We went to the funeral home to see him, and it made cold chills run all over me to know that he was one of the people who got me started working with the horses.

The funeral home where they had Buford's funeral, was just across the street from the gas station where I was working. It was like I was inside, because I could hear what was going on. His passing made me very sad. He was a very good friend.

I had a few days off work, so I drove out to the fair grounds. I wanted to see what it looked like after being gone for a few years. It hadn't changed very much, it still looked about the same. I sure had a lot of memories of that place.

While I was there I run into an old friend. His name was Jerry lee. He had two horses that he wanted to take to Miles Park race track for a few weeks. As soon as he saw me I think bells went off in his head. He asked me if I would be interested in taking the horses to the track for a few weeks.

I didn't really know what to do, but I knew that I would see a lot of horse people at the track, and I thought that might be a good thing. I told Jerry that I didn't have a trainer's license, and he said that I would have to take a test. He said it shouldn't be very hard to pass.

I went home and talked to Norma, and she really didn't want me to do it. Jerry told me I could drive back and forth every day, and there would be days that I wouldn't have to go at all, because he had a man that was going to stay down at the track to take care of the horses. I thought it might be good to get away for a while.

I couldn't stay gone very long at a time since Norma was pregnant, and getting bigger every day. I knew that while I was working for Jerry the money would be good. His father owned a night club in Lebanon called The Golden Horse Shoe. It was a real nice place.

Jerry had a cousin named Dickie Lee that spent the summer in Lebanon. He was about the same age as me. I didn't see Dickie any more for a lot of years. One day I was watching television on a country music station, and I saw Dickie playing guitar and singing. I had no idea that he was a singer.

The day we shipped the horses to Miles Park, I drove down behind the horse van. We had no problems, and after we got the horses set up in their stalls, I had to go to the racing office to check on taking my trainers test. I had to talk to the stewards, and they gave me a date to come back and take the test. It really didn't bother me, because I thought I knew what I needed to know to pass the test.

The next few days we were getting one of the horses ready to run. His name was Colonel Lee. They thought he was a real nice horse. On the day that I had to take the test I had to be there early. The test took over two hours. After I finished I turned the test in to the stewards. They took a little time to look it over, but it wasn't long before Mr. Findley came out and told me that I did quite well on the test. He congratulated me and wished me good luck. I should have been excited, but I wasn't, because my heart was set on being a blacksmith.

Now that I had my trainer's license I could enter Colonel Lee in a race. It wasn't but a couple of days until a race come up for him to run in. I entered him and he got in. I knew that Mr. Lee would be down to watch him run.

The next day we needed some supplies from Becker and Durski turf supply, and Mr. Lee drove me over there. After we got what we needed, the owner of the store started talking to me. He knew that I had worked at Pinkstons Turf Shop in Lexington, Ky., and that Pinkstons was the only place that you could get name plates made that went on the horse's halter.

Raymond Griffith asked me if I knew where a name plate jig could be found, and I told him that I could make him one. I had to convince him that I could really make one. He finally told me if I could make a name plate jig, that he would pay good money for it. I explained that I went back and forth from Lebanon every few days, and when I got it made I would drop it off to him. He thanked me, and I went back to Miles Park to run Colonel Lee.

When his race finally come up, Colonel Lee actually run very good. He finished third, but he only got beat a couple of lengths. Mr. Lee was very pleased.

In the next few weeks I started to work on Mr. Griffith's name plate jig. I had to get a man in Lebanon to help me, because I had the know how, but I didn't have the tools to do the job. I drew the man a blueprint, but it took a couple of weeks before he had time to make it. When he called me to come and pick it up, I couldn't believe how good a job he did. Mr. Griffith would be pleased.

The next trip I made to Miles Park, I stopped by Becker & Durski. Mr. Griffith was more than pleased with the way it looked. He still had to buy a couple of different sized dies. He was even more pleased that I only charged him forty dollars to make it.

We didn't have a very long stay at Miles Park. Colonel Lee bowed a tendon in his leg, and the other horses never did get to start. I chalked that one up to experience. The last time I was in Luckett Tack Shop I saw my jig setting up on a shelf. I don't know if Mr. Luckett knows who made it or not.

Norma's brother-in-law, who owned a tile company, asked me if I would like to go to work for him. I thought that I might like the tile business, so I told him that I would. We had found a house just outside of town. The rent wasn't very much, and the kids had a yard to play in.

My brother-in-law's name was Louis Watson, and he was married to Norma's oldest sister. Louis was a pretty good guy, just set in his ways. We didn't work on the weekend, so that gave me some time to do some blacksmith work. Louis did tile work all over the country, so I was able to meet a lot of people. A lot of the people that we worked for had horses. I knew it would take me a while to build up some blacksmith work, but I knew it would happen.

As I got into the tile business, I caught on very quickly. Later on, I realized that tile work was a form of art, and so was blacksmithing. After a few weeks. I asked Louis how long it would take for me to learn to lay tile. He told me that it usually took about two years. I sure fooled him. In three months, I was laying as much tile as he was. There was still a lot of things that I didn't know, but I really did enjoy learning about the business. Sometimes I think Louis was jealous, because I made three times more money on the weekend shoeing horses, than I made all week working for him. I finally felt like I was on the right road.

Louis and I was working in Danville, Kentucky one day, and we saw a nineteen forty Plymouth, that was for sale. I went back on the weekend and bought it. The man said that the motor wasn't any good, so I got the car cheap. In a few weeks, I found a motor, and Bobby Isham helped me change the motor in the car. I used the car on the weekend, to work out of, while I was shoeing horses.

I didn't keep the car very long, because while I was working in Columbia, Kentucky, I found a Dodge panel truck. I talked to the car salesman for a while, and I knew that he really wanted my Plymouth. He finally agreed to trade the two cars even. We fixed the papers on the truck, and I drove it back to Lebanon. The truck drove good, and I realized that it was a three quarter ton, and had a lot of room in it. I could put shelves and a forge in the back, and that would keep all my blacksmith equipment dry.

I did a good job of fixing up my truck. My uncle gave me a small forge, and an old anvil. That was enough to get me started. As I worked, I accumulated quite a few tools, and in those days, almost every hardware store carried horse shoes in stock. I also learned about Stockhoff's in Louisville, Kentucky. It was a horseshoe supply store.

After I got everything pretty well set up, I started branching out with my blacksmith business. I went to Columbia, where I still knew a lot of people from riding at the fair. I also went to Russell Springs, Kentucky. I knew a lot of people everywhere I went. The last place I went was to Somerset, Kentucky. I ran into a gentleman who I desperately needed to know. His name was Elmer Humphrey, and he run a big walking horse operation.

Elmer was different than any other horse person that I knew. I had met a lot of good horsemen, but none like Elmer. He told me that I could come and go, anytime I could get there. He said that he always had young horses to work on, night or day. He also knew that I wasn't experienced in shoeing walking horses, so I would have to learn as I went along.

When I first started going to Elmer's farm, he would take a horse out of the stall, and tie it to the cross ties. He had a blackboard set up next to the horse that he would write the angles on that he wanted on the horses' feet, and then he would walk away, and not bother me while I was shoeing the horse. Elmer did a really good job of training his horses, and he was also good to the people who worked for him. He was a natural at what he did. He also gave me some tools that was used to shoe walking horses.

After I started going to different places on the weekend, I had such a good feeling about shoeing horses. I worked in that part of the country for the rest of the year, and got through the winter by working in the tile business for Louis. By the next spring, I had enough work to make a living shoeing horses. I knew that if I didn't, I could always go back to laying tile, but I thought that I could make it.

Once I started shoeing a lot of walking horses, I found a big forge in Lebanon. The forge weighted nearly three hundred pounds, so I had to get a man with a pickup truck to move it. I put it in the blacksmith shop at the fair grounds, in Lebanon. When I got everything set up in the blacksmith shop, I started making walking horse shoes every Saturday. I really got good at making the shoes, and I started taking them to Lexington, and selling them to Breeder's Supply. I really liked knowing that my shoes were being used by other blacksmiths.

Later on Bobby and I would get together at his house, and practice making all kinds of horseshoes. I knew that what I was doing was very good training, plus, Bobby might wind up being a blacksmith, also. It would be something, having two self-made blacksmiths, from the same town. Bobby worked for the light company, but I knew that he wanted to be a blacksmith. It was the first time in a long time that I woke up in the middle of the night and wanted to get up and go to work.

Norma went to the doctor and found out that her due date was in July. That would make three out of four of our kids born in July. At least we were consistent. We were going to Somerset, Kentucky the next weekend, and Norma decided to go with me. We were going to work at Elmer's farm all day. They were more like family than someone that you worked for. We had already put in a full day's work, when a gentleman came by the farm and asked if I could stop by his place and shoe his horse before we went home. He said that he was going on a trail ride that weekend, and really needed the horse shod. I told him that it would probably be dark by the time we got to his place, and he said that was OK, I could shoe the horse in the dark.

By the time we got there it was dark. The only thing you could see was the outline of a horse standing there, but I got my tools, and put some shoes on the horse.

The next time I went to Elmer's to shoe horses, I stopped by to see what the horse looked like that I had shod in the dark. It actually looked pretty good. I was very proud. It had started being about the horse and not about how much money I could make. I always had a different outlook on the horses than most people did.

Another time while I was working at Elmer's, a man came by the barn and wanted to know if I could come to his place and trim his mare. He said that he was taking her to a horse show. I thought that it was odd that anyone would show a mare without putting shoes on her. The man told me where to come, and said not to be surprised at what I saw. When I got to the man's farm, I was shocked. The mare had six legs. Two legs in the back, and four legs in the front. I could never have imagined a horse being that way, but I trimmed her without any trouble. The man asked me to come by his place and trim the mare several times, while I was working in that area. He took her to several shows every summer, so people could come by and see her. It was quite different seeing a horse like her. I realized, that if I lived to be a hundred, I will never see it all.

I started going to Russell Springs, Kentucky regularly to shoe horses for Larry Holt. I had met Larry a few summers back, and now he had started training a few horses. On one of my trips, Larry told me that he had gotten a horse in his barn that I used to ride when I was an exercise rider. He said that his exercise boy was having a hard time galloping the horse, and I told Larry that I couldn't believe he was hard to gallop, because when I rode him he was really nice to gallop.

I told Larry that the next time I came back to shoe his horses, that I would bring my boots and gallop the horse for him. Larry said OK, so the following week I went back to Larry's and brought my boots with me.

They got the horse ready to gallop, and when they brought the horse out in the shed row, Larry gave me a leg up in the saddle. The horse walked off like he always did for me. I jogged him off, and he broke into a gallop. I let the reins stay loose, he galloped three times around Russell Springs race track without any problems. Larry could not believe it.

No telling how many times I have seen Larry Holt in the last thirty years. He never forgets to say something about that day.

I knew that I had to start thinking about Norma. It wouldn't be long until she had our fourth child. Our other kids were already wanting to go to grandmaw's house. One day I was working in Russell Springs, Kentucky, and the people where I was working had the radio on. I heard them say that Mr. Fitzsimmons had died. I sat down on the back of my truck, and the man holding the horse for me to shoe, asked me what was wrong. I told him that I had worked for Mr. Fitz a couple of years before, and that he was a super horseman, and a legend, and he will certainly be missed. I couldn't keep from crying a little. Then I went back to work.

In a few days I took Norma to her mother's house. In less than a week our fourth child was born. We had a big girl, and we named her Terry Lynn. She was born on July twenty-first, nineteen sixty four. After Terry was born, I was worried about where we lived. It was nice in the summer, but if we stayed in the winter, we would have to burn wood. We needed to find a house in town, where the babies wouldn't have to be around a wood stove. While the baby was getting a little older, we would try to find a better place to live.

With winter coming there was another problem. A lot of the people that I was working for would shut down the horse part of their operation. I didn't know how that was going to work. We found a house in town, close to where Norma went to high school, and it was a nice place. When the horse shoeing did die down in the winter, Norma went to work at Angel Manufacturing Company. Our house was two story, and we rented the upstairs apartment out. That helped to get us through the winter months. In the spring, the man who owned the house told us that he sold it, and that we would have to move.

We lucked up on another house just a few blocks from where we were living. Our family helped us move. We still didn't have a lot of furniture, so it didn't take us very long to move. It was hard that winter. I went to work a half block up the street from our house, at a flooring company, to help out. It was just for the winter. I hadn't worked there very long, when the workers went on strike. I still got a small check all winter, even though they were on strike. That lasted all winter.

When spring broke, I finally started shoeing a few horses. When I got a few extra dollars, I ordered a pair of G. E. nippers. They were hand made, and cost forty dollars a pair. They were the Cadillac of nippers. Shortly after that, I was in Goshen, Kentucky, and I run in to Dravo Foley. He knew that I was shoeing horses, and he said that he had about forty mares and babies on the farm that needed to be trimmed. He wanted me to come as soon as possible and do them. I told him that I would be there the next week. I had to make a couple of trips to get them all done. As soon as I was finished, Davo gave me a check. That was the biggest lick I had ever made at one time.

As soon as Dravo paid me, he wanted to know if I would go to work for him full time. He offered me a house, and twelve hundred dollars a month, plus I could do the shoeing on my own time. I told Dravo that I would talk to Norma about it and let him know. When I got back home, I told Norma about what was going on. I think she said, "here we go again", but not out loud. After we talked about it for a while, we decided that the offer was hard to turn down.

David, Jr., our oldest child, was in the first grade. We knew that the Oldham county school system was the best in the state. After a lot of hard thinking, I realized we knew a lot of horse people in that area. Even if the job with Dravo didn't work out, I could shoe a lot of horses in that area. I called Dravo and told him that I might consider going to work for him, but my family couldn't come until school was out for the summer. Dravo said that would be fine, so I loaded some things in my truck, and went to work.

When I got there, it was on the weekend. Dravo had several people working there at the barn, and I thought everything was good. On Monday morning when I went to work, there wasn't another person on that farm, but me. I called Dravo to find out what was going on. He told me that I was the farm manager, and I would have to find some help. I should have gone home right then. It took about three weeks to get enough help to run the farm and training center. All the people that I saw when I came to work, was the weekend help. Most of them were Dravo's relatives. I was disappointed at how everything started out, but I was determined to make it work.

Dravo's wife was having a lot of work done on our house, and I thought in time things might work out. After school was out in Lebanon, and Norma and the kids got moved in, things were a lot easier. I thought it just wouldn't work that way, but in just a few days after Norma and the kids got moved in, I went to work one morning, and the only help I had to run the training center, was two young boys. I called Norma, and told her to come over to the training center. When she got there, I told her that she would have to walk some horses, to cool them out, after they come from the race track. Norma liked to have had a fit. She had never walked any race horses, but she finally tried, and was very good at it. After that day, I had to call her quite often. Dravo was always gone. He spent the summer at River Downs Race Track in Ohio.

I also wound up with another job that I didn't know about. Every once in a while, we would switch the horses from the training center to River Downs to run. I would take them up at night on the horse van, and wouldn't get back home until eleven or twelve o'clock. Then I would have to get up at five o'clock and start all over again. This went on seven days a week. When I got through work in the afternoon, I would shoe horses until dark. I did this for three or four days a week. I was a busy man, but the money was good.

Dravo told me to get a small beef calf, and he would furnish the feed for it until it was big enough to butcher. We also had a big garden, but I didn't have much time to work in it. I felt good about the first five horses that I took to River Downs from the training center. They all won the first time they run, and two of them won stake races. They were Brave Beau, and Vickies Choice. They were very nice horses. It didn't take long for the summer to be gone. When September came around, we would have two children in school. It didn't seem possible.

One of the best things about living in Oldham County. There was a lot of activity for the kids. There was a lot of fall things going on at the school, which was only a half mile from where we lived. The school and church was right in the front of the training center where I worked. It was only a little way from Mr. Hilliard's farm where I worked at before, so we already knew a lot of people in the area. There was also a lot of horses around, and I thought this might just be the best spot in Kentucky to be a blacksmith. There wasn't any competition, and it was only twenty minutes to Louisville. Hopefully the next few years would be good for us. There is one good thing about working at a training center. It never shuts down.

Dravo had sent a horse down to the farm from River Downs for a little T.L.C. The horse had been there for about a month, and it was getting to be county fair time. I still missed going to the fair, and riding in the races.

One day while we were talking, I told Dravo that we should take Carolyns Pine to the fair and enter him in a race. He said that we might take him to the fair, if I would ride him. I told him that I would, but I really thought that would be the last I heard about it.

Dravo was getting ready to go back to River Downs, and on Monday, he told me to get Carolyns Pine up out of the field and start galloping him. I started galloping the horse the next week, and he was really hard to gallop.

When Dravo came home the next week, we started making plans to go to the fair. He said we could take the horse on our horse van and leave him at the fair all week. Someone was going to drive down with us to bring us back to the farm. Norma was going with me. She had never been involved with the horses at the fair.

We left the training center early morning on the first day of the fair. When we got there and got the horse unloaded, and settled down, I had a strange feeling come over me. I hadn't had that feeling in a long time. The first thing I did was get me some cotton candy.

There was a full day of races that day at the fair. They had pony races, and mule races, and one thoroughbred race. The thoroughbred race was the last race of the day.

It seemed like it took forever for the last race to get there. I got dressed and put my boots on. Dravo had sent a set of his racing colors to run in. When the horses came out on the track, Carolyns Pine seemed to be calm. The only thing I was worried about, was that he had never started without a starting gate.

All the horses lined up, and I was a little behind the other horses. The starter yelled for me to come on down with the other horses. I clucked to Carolyns Pine, and broke him off, and the starter said "go". Before I got to the first turn, we were three links in front of the rest of the horses. Carolyns Pine was much the best horse. Needless to say, we Won.

We had to go back to Oldham County and work the next day, but we had people staying at the fair to take care of the horse. That is where Dravo was from, and everybody knew everybody.

We had to wait until Saturday to run again. The race was called the Russel County Derby. It was a big deal to win the derby, but our luck didn't hold out. We got everything ready on Derby day, and when they threw me up on the horse, he didn't seem like the same horse I rode on Wednesday.

He was broke out in a sweat, and his coat was solid white. When we got close to the other horses on the track, he broke off and I went twice around the track. I couldn't stop him. I finally turned him into the back gate, and got him off the race track.

The other horses went on and run the race. It was a disappointing trip home for us. We like to never got him cooled out, and I could have gotten killed. I think somebody gave him too much dope!

One day Dravo told me that he was going to have a partner. His name was Holman Wilson, and they were going to call the training center Woodacre Farm. Dravo said that Mr. Wilson owned channel thirty two television station, and it sounded like he would be a good partner. I know over time Mr. Wilson helped me a lot. Sometimes he would disagree with Dravo, but Mr. Wilson was sharp.

We were sitting in the barn talking one day, and I told Mr. Wilson that I had written a song, but we didn't know where to go to get it published. He said that his son was in that business, and where I could find him in Nashville, Tennessee. In a few weeks when Dravo came home, we took a couple of days off, and went to Nashville. We called Mr. Wilson's son, and he told us to bring the tape to his office, and he would listen to it. After he listened to the tape, he sent us to Surefire Publishing Company, and told us to ask for Bill Brock. Norma sung the song for Mr. Brock, and the company published it. That was quite an experience, and somewhat different from being a blacksmith.

Because of the help problem, Dravo had me galloping a lot of horses every day. We also had a lot of yearlings to break. I didn't know if I could last at this pace. I was only human. I was doing the work of four people, and Dravo would say it was all in a day's work. The only thing that Dravo ever did was sweep the shedrow. He was a hall of fame sweeper.

I hung in there until winter was over, then Dravo went back to Ohio with the horses. Things were going a little better, but then breeding season started, and he wanted me to take the mares to be bred between everything else that I had to do. This went on until I just couldn't do it any longer. I told Dravo that I was through. I told him that I would get on some horses and do the shoeing, and he agreed. We found a house even closer to work than the one we lived in. When you can do a lot of things, people expect you to do too much, even though the money was good.

My brother came to see us one day, and he said that one of his friends wanted to give me half interest in a horse, if I would break and train it. I called the man, and he told me where the horse was. When we went to pick the horse up, there was something that they hadn't told us. The horse wasn't broke to lead, or anything. He was running out in a corn field with his mother. I'm not sure if the horse had ever seen a person. It took us hours to get him loaded, but we finally got him home. It took a while, but he finally calmed down, and trusted Norma. I didn't have all the extra work now, so I had a little time to work with the horse.

There was a corn crib on Woodacre Farm that Dravo didn't have anything to do with. I called Mr. Axton, who owned the farm, and he said that I could use the building, free. I made a stall on one side of the building, and used the other side to keep my hay and straw. It really worked out well.

Mr. Browning owned the other half of the horse, and he sent me the horse's papers. The horse's name was J. C. Comet. It would be a long process before he run, but he did catch on to what he was supposed to do, very quickly. He was really smart, and after about a month, we had him galloping a little. When I got through work every morning, I would gallop him.

One morning Dravo asked me if I could come back to the barn later that day, and help them load some sale yearlings on the van, that was going to Florida. I told him that I would be there at four o'clock. When I came back, the van was backed up to the doors of the barn so the yearlings couldn't get out of the barn. It was very slow work trying to load the yearlings. We got to one that did not want to load. Someone handed me a scoop shovel, and told me to make a little noise behind the filly. All of a sudden she backed up enough to kick the shovel with both feet, and hit the end of the shovel around my hand.

I looked down, and my fingers were hanging down at least three inches lower than they were supposed to be, and one of my knuckles was gone. It made me very sick, I guess that I was in shock. They took me to the hospital in LaGrange, Kentucky. The doctor in the emergency room put a roll of gauze in my hand, and taped it, because the person who run the x-ray machine wasn't there. They gave me some pain pills, and told me to come back the next day.

The next morning, Norma took me back to the hospital, and when they x-rayed my hand, they told me that I should go to Jewish Hospital, in Louisville, Kentucky, and see Dr. Kutz and Dr. Kleinert. They said that someone from the hospital would call them while we were on our way there. It took several hours to prepare me to fix my hand, and it took several hours to put my hand back together. When the doctor came in the next day, he told me that it looked bad, but he knew that I was a horse person, and horse people were tough. He said it would be left up to me how well it worked.

I would have to do a lot of therapy on my own. I was worried about my insurance, but I had worker's compensation, and they would take care of the hospital bill. I was told that I would draw one hundred and sixty dollars a month, and that wasn't much, compared to the fifteen hundred dollars a month that I was used to making.

I was determined to get through this. I had a lot of will power, and a good woman. I knew it would be rough, and I had to figure out what we were going to do. I knew that we couldn't live where we were. We had to look around for something that we could afford. I don't know how Norma found this house. It was right in the edge of LaGrange. It was cheap, but it wasn't very good. I knew that we would have to make out with it.

The boys at the farm where I was working said that they would take care of our horse for awhile, so not to worry about him. This changed my whole way of thinking. I had heard about the Supreme Court ruling that blacksmiths couldn't be union in Kentucky. I had talked to the head of the blacksmith union, Vick Gushay, that fall, and he told me that he would give me a blacksmith test in the spring. I knew that this would mess that up. I would just have to see what worked out.

In a few weeks, Dr. Kutz called and said for me to come to his office and he would take the pins out of my fingers. That wasn't very pleasant. It hurt a lot, because he just took hold of the pins and pulled them out. The doc looked at my hand, and said that it looked good. He told me that he had to take my knuckle out, because it was knocked all the way through my hand. He gave me three different sized rubber balls, to start doing therapy with, on my hand.

As the weeks went on, I tried to work hard to get my hand working, but it wasn't easy. The worse part was that there wasn't much income. Norma started walking horses at the training barn, that way she could also keep an eye on our horse. He looked forward to Norma coming to the barn every morning. He was a very smart horse, and he was the last thing that we needed right now. You just don't know from one day to the next what might happen.

I knew that it would take about all summer for me to be able to shoe horses again. When Miles Park Race Track opened for training, I got a friend to take our horse to the race track. I knew that I could take care of one horse, but a miracle happened. Doug Davis, my old boss, moved a big stable of horses in to the track. After he found out about my hand being broke, he asked me if I could ride the pony. I told him that I could, and he said he needed a pony boy to walk to and from the race track, with his young horses.

Mr. Davis put me on salary. It had to be a miracle for a person in my shape to be able to get a job. It actually was good therapy for my hand using the bridle reigns. I knew it wouldn't hurt anything, and Norma kept working for Dravo. At least the two of us together could make enough money to feed the kids.

When the races started, Dodge Ferguson moved some horses into the same barn as Mr. Davis. He knew about our situation, and he wanted Norma to start walking horses for them. We could all be together during training hours, and the kids could play in the tack room. We could at least get by, and the kids seemed to like the horses. I knew if I could make it through Ellis Park race meet, that I could start back shoeing horses. When the time came to move to Ellis Park I started asking around, and it seemed like everyone was willing to help us.

I run into Jack Fuchs one morning, and he said that I could use one of his stalls for our horse until I could find another one. Then in a day or two, I run into Mr. Vangorp. He said that he would ship our horse on his van with some other horses, and wouldn't charge us anything. That was the way that people used to be. Now that we had the horse taken care of, we had to try to get us taken care of, and get us there. At least our car was in pretty good shape.

We finally got everything moved to Ellis Park, and I was hoping to have some luck. When we got there, I went to Jack Fuchs' barn and checked on the horse. Then I drove around the barn area, and somebody told me that Oran Battles might need a groom. I went to Mr. Battles' barn and he told me that he had a groom who was supposed to come to work the next day, but if he didn't come, then I could have the job. I asked him about a stall for our horse, and he said that he had an empty stall. We just had to wait until tomorrow.

I went to Mr. Battles' barn early the next morning. The other groom didn't show up, so I got the job. He showed me the three horses that I would be grooming, and the empty stall was right next to those horses. I thought that would be perfect. Mr. Battles asked what my wife was going to be doing, and I told him that I really didn't know. He asked if she wanted to walk horses, and she jumped at the chance. He asked me where we were going to live, and I told him that I really didn't know.

Mr. Battles called Ruth Adkins, the lady who run the race track, and she came to the barn and talked to us. She said that they had outside buildings for tack rooms, and she would have them put two rooms together for us to live in. The shower and bathrooms were right beside the barn, and Ruth told the guards to keep close check on us and the kids every night. Norma was the first female to ever live on a race track in Kentucky.

Mr. Battles had seventeen horses at the race track, and he was a super horseman. He was an Oklahoma cowboy, and very quiet. He was always watching the other horses train on the race track.

We hadn't been there but a couple of days, when a man brought a bunch of tomatoes and corn to the barn. His name was Mr. Jackson. He had a horse in the barn, also, and he said that he had two sons. One of them had been a rider for awhile, and rode a few races, but now they just worked with the horses in the mornings, since they both had other jobs. Their names were Mike and Bob Jackson. Bob worked in the office at Ellis Park, for the race track.

After the races started, the three horses that I groomed, all won. Westark won his first race, and when he run his second race, he won again. Norma got paid extra for walking the winner and after the first week, we thought we were rich. The best part was that my hand was getting better every day. Almost every day someone would cook out, and everyone was invited. There was watermelon and cantaloupe everywhere. It was like being at a big country fair. It was a wonderful time.

One day Mr. Battles asked me if I had seen Vick Gusha, the blacksmith. We had been there for three weeks, and he hadn't been by the barn to check the horses' shoes. Mr. Battles said that he needed some horses shod. I told him that I hadn't seen Vick, but I had my shoeing box with me, and I could shoe two or three if he wanted me to. He said wait until the next day, that he might be able to find Vick.

By the next day Vick still hadn't showed up, so Mr. Battles showed me which horses to shoe. About half way through the first horse that I shod, Vick showed up. He got out of his car, and steam was flying off his ears. He wanted to know what I was doing shoeing a horse at the race track. Mr. Battles told Vick that he had been waiting for him for three weeks, so he was letting me shoe the horses. Vick told Mr. Battles that he was going to turn him in to the race track stewards. The stewards called Mr. Battles into the office for a meeting. When the meeting was over, they told Vick Gusha that they should fine him for not showing up on time.

After that everything went pretty smooth. We run our horse, J. C. Comet, and he didn't run very good. Mr. Battles said that we run him for too much money, and we probably did. We were going to run him once more at Ellis Park, because after that meet was over, Norma would have to go home and put the kids back in school. I guessed that I would go with Mr. Battles to Turfway Park. I thought about selling the horse, because we weren't in a position to have a horse. We had made a little money at Ellis Park, but it was not like me working as a blacksmith.

While I was working for Mr. Battles, I run in to a colorful person, again. It was little John Adams, Jr. He was working for Mr. Battles as an exercise boy. I had met John before, when I was working as an outrider at Keeneland. John had some bad luck with his family, and he said that he had to drink to get by. He told me a heartbreaking story. He said that when his father, John Adams, Sr., was riding races, they were moving to California. Little John was a baby, and his mother was driving across country with him in the car. Somewhere along the way, she run off the road down a steep embankment. Little John's mother was killed, and he was in the car with her for several days before any one found them. That was a very heart wrenching story. When Little John was riding races, he was one of the leading riders in the country. It was a pleasure to know someone like that.

Just a few days before the end of Ellis Park races, we run J. C. Comet again. He didn't run any better this time. Norma got everything together, and took the kids home so they could start school. Mr. Vangorp took

J. C. Comet to Turfway Park for me. After we were at Turfway for a few days, a man offered to buy him for twenty five hundred dollars. I told him that I would take it. We only got half the money, because Mr. Browning owned half of him.

After I sold the horse, I didn't stay at Turfway Park very long. Norma had to drive up there on the weekends, and I didn't have any way to get around, or get food. I told Mr. Battles that I was going home. I knew there wasn't very much to do at home, after I went. After I was home for a few days, we drove to Goshen, Kentucky. I saw Dravo Foley, and he said that he needed a man to work on his broodmare farm. I told him that I would take the job. Dravo lent me his horse van, and we moved our furniture to a house just down the hill from where I was going to work. I thought something good would have to happen soon. I worked there all winter, and in to the start of spring.

Norma and I talked it over a few times about me quitting, and trying something different. Each time we talked, Norma would say that she didn't know what I could do to make enough money to keep everything going. Then another miracle happened. J. H. VanWert came to our house one morning, and wanted to hire me. I told him that I was working. He said, "no", I want you to shoe my horses. He said that he was tired of his blacksmith not showing up half the time. He said he had some good owners, like J. Graham Brown, one of the richest men in the county.

Mr. VanWert said that he would pay me as soon as I gave him a bill every month. He said that I could start the next day, and I told him that I would be there. I told Norma that our luck was changing, thank God. I worked there for a while, and it was a good job. There was a lot of horses to trim, and quite a few to shoe. It was a nice amount each month. I didn't want to overload my hand.

It really surprised me when Dravo came down to Mr. VanWert's farm. I thought that he was just visiting, but he asked me if I could shoe some horses for him, and I said that I would. As the summer went on, I kept picking up new people to shoe for. It certainly looked better than it had. With no bad luck, we should be OK.

The place where we lived had a large garden. I had gotten the kids a little pony, and they were tickled to death. We also had some chickens, and some meat hogs. When July came, it was like my world ended. My grandfather Gribbins died. That was really hard for me. He was the one who got me started with the horses. We went to his funeral. He was such a good man. The church was full of people. This was where I was raised, and it was so sad, but you have to go on. I know that he was proud of his grandchildren.

After the funeral, I went back to work. There was one good thing about working for Mr. VanWert and Dravo. The work didn't end in the winter. It might slow up some, but I was in better shape than I had ever been. I thought it had to get better. I was interested in getting my blacksmith license so that I could shoe horses at the race track.

When Churchill Downs fall race meet started, I went to the race track and looked up Vick Gusha and talked to him. He told me that he would give me a shoeing test in the spring. It had been two years since the Supreme Court ruled on the blacksmith union in Kentucky, so I thought that Vick was messing me around. After next spring, I was going to do something about it. Actually, I wasn't hardly ready in my own mind. I didn't want to make any mistakes. I had been too long getting here, and I had certainly enjoyed everything that I had learned. Some people want to shoe horses too quick, and it doesn't work. You have to know what you are doing.

I really enjoyed working at the VanWert farm. It gave me a sense of security. Mr. VanWert had a huge barn inside area of the farm. I didn't know what they used the barn for. It used to be for their broodmare operations, but they didn't use it for that any more. I found out that Ronnie Warren had moved some of his lay up horses in to the barn, and after awhile I started to do some work for him. The work was mostly trimming the horses, but over the next several years I worked for him at several different places.

I was always running into people who wanted a horse shod. That winter Ernest Craycraft called me, and said that he run a horse farm for Billy Reynolds. He said that he had some horses that needed to be shod. The farm was just outside LaGrange, Kentucky, so I decided to go to the farm and check it out. It was a big, nice farm. Ernest said that Mr. Reynolds didn't want nippers used on his horses, just the rasp and the knife to trim out the feet. He said that I would still get paid the full amount for trimming the horses, the only problem was that it was slow pay.

I didn't realize it for a while, but Mr. VanWert was the one who called Ernest and told him about me. That made two big farms that I would be working for this winter. Even though it was cold, and we had a lot of snow, it was a good winter. This was the first winter that I didn't have to get another job just to make ends meet.

As soon as Churchill Downs opened for its spring race meet, I was going to see Vick Gusha about getting my blacksmith license, because Mr. VanWert's son, Billy, always took horses to Churchill to run in the races. They wanted me to shoe their horses at Churchill, but I couldn't work at the track without a license. I went to the track and looked up Vick, but he told me the same thing that he always did. He said that he would give me a test to get my license in the fall. I didn't know exactly how, but I was going to outfox Mr. Gusha.

All that year I talked to different people about what was going on in the blacksmith union. I finally realized that I had a horse friend in Lebanon, Kentucky. His name was H. P. Morancy, and he worked in the licensing department for the racing commission. I went to the racing office and talked to Mr. Morancy. He told me that he really didn't know what was going on, but he would try to find out.

Mr. Morancy was a good friend of ex-governor, Happy Chandler, so he called Happy to see what I should do. Happy told Mr. Morancy to set up a governor's test for me. It took a little while, but they did set up the test for me at Churchill Downs. They got two trainers, a blacksmith, and a veterinarian to watch me shoe a horse. Everyone had known me for so long, and knew that I could shoe horses, that they were surprised that I even had to take a test. I passed the test, and went to the racing office and got my blacksmith license. I was very proud of it. I couldn't believe that it had taken me four years to get it.

It took from nineteen sixty four to nineteen sixty eight. It seemed like everything that I did took a long time, except getting married. One of the trainers who watched me take my test, was Ray Frazer. He had wanted me to shoe his horses for a long time, but I couldn't, because I didn't have a license.

I only wanted to pick up a few horses to shoe at the race track. I just wanted to be there enough so people could see me and know that I could shoe at the track. Most of my work was in Oldham County, but I knew as time went on, things would change. The horse business was starting to get good in Oldham County. There wasn't much change in my life for the next couple of years, except my work.

I couldn't believe our oldest son was already nine years old. He had started going to work with me, and I couldn't believe how talented he was. It seemed like he already knew how to shoe a horse. Everyone on the race track knew him, and liked him. He was learning a lesson for his future.

Since I was always wanting to do something to improve the business, I had made a drawing of an aluminum shoeing box. As far as I knew, there had never been one made before. We had a large garden that year with super big tomatoes. There was a boat factory right across the road from where we lived. The people from the boat factory could see our garden from their window. One day a gentleman from the factory came walking over toward the garden. He introduced himself as Mr. Pluckenbaum, and wanted to know if he could buy some of our tomatoes. I told him no, but I would give him all the tomatoes that he wanted. I think that it surprised him, and he said if there was ever anything that he could do for us, to just let him know.

For some reason, I had the drawing of the aluminum shoeing box in my pocket. I handed it to Mr. Pluckenbaum, and asked him if he could make the box. He looked at the drawing and said that he was sure he could make it. I told him to make two boxes, and he said to give him a few days, and he would make them in his spare time. In a few days he came over to the house with the boxes. Norma got a grocery bag and picked him a big bag of tomatoes, since he wouldn't take any money for the boxes. I was sure enough proud of my shoeing boxes. I knew that the aluminum shoeing box had just been born. I found out that something else in our life was going to be born. Norma had just found out that she was pregnant again. Maybe this time we would get a baby for Christmas.

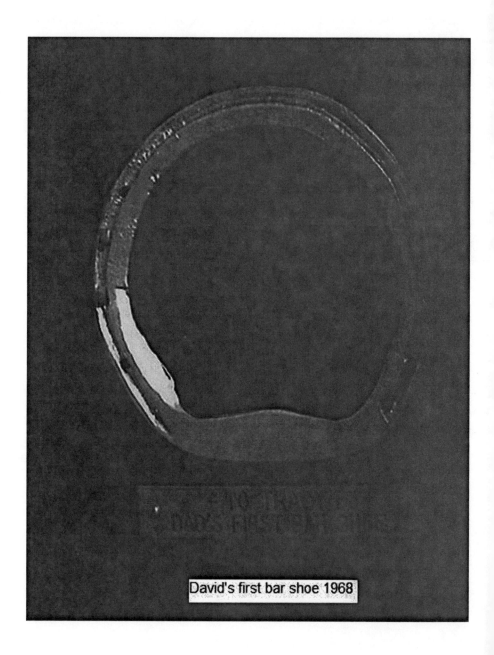

David's first bar shoe 1968

Every blacksmith that saw my shoeing box wanted to buy one, or wanted to know where they could get one like it. All the blacksmiths were carrying heavy wooden boxes, and my box was small, light, and balanced. Even though it had just been made, I had been carrying the drawing of it in my pocket for a couple of years. There had never been any other shoeing boxes made of aluminum. I know that everywhere I went to work, everybody paid attention to my shoeing box.

I was always hoping that things would work out. I wanted to try to work for people who had a lot of horses in one place. Sometimes you can get strung out driving too far, and not doing enough work to come out even. I had met one of Mr. VanWert's exercise boys, his name was George Ogle, and I knew him from when I worked in New Jersey. George said that he had moved to Kentucky to try to start training horses. He said that he was going to gallop horses for Mr. VanWert for a while, so he could make some connections with some of the trainers and owners.

It had been a pretty good summer, and I couldn't ask for anything more. Now I was looking forward to our fifth child, and to Christmas, but our son was born on December the first. We named him Daniel Cleo. That sounded like a blacksmith to me, Daniel Cleo Wilson. Now we had three girls, and two blacksmiths. Our other son, David, Jr., was eleven years old, and it wouldn't be long before he would be shoeing horses.

We made it through the cold weather pretty good. We had a lot of sleet and ice. I had to stay at home a few times because of the weather, but it was starting to warm up some, and spring is always welcome to horse people. I felt that since I had some more experience shoeing at the race track now, Churchill Downs spring meet would be a good one for me. When they started letting the horses in at Churchill, I picked up a few small stables of horses to shoe. The other blacksmiths weren't very friendly, but that was normal. I would change that, but it would take time.

Opening day at Churchill Downs grew near, and Churchill is such an exciting place to be at Derby time. After the derby was over, Blacky

Huffman, the farm manager for Triple R. Farm, asked me if I could come by the farm, and shoe a couple of horses that he was going to run at Churchill Downs. I told him that I would come the next day, and over the next couple of y ears, I did quite a few horses at Triple R. Farm.

When the spring meet was over at Churchill, the Miles Park meet opened. It was just across town, in Louisville, Kentucky, and was getting to be a popular little race track. As soon as I started working there, I run into Donald Hughes. He had twelve horses. I had met Donald when I first started galloping horses at Lexington, Kentucky. It was the start of a long working relationship. It seemed that every day I met someone at the race track that I knew. Ray Frazer shipped in to the race track with twelve horses. He wanted me to do his work. Kenny Burkhart was a first time job. I also run in to a quiet little gentleman that asked me about shoeing horses, but he didn't exactly ask me to shoe a horse. His name was Jimmy Hikes. I knew that he was a little different, but he just didn't know me. Thirty years down the road he was one of the smartest trainers that I ever knew. I also knew his brother, who was a trainer, too. His name was Johnny Hikes. They were quiet, but their brain was always working. They were both super people.

George Ogle told me that he had picked up three horses to train, and for me not to let him down when he wanted them shod. I told him to just holler when he needed something. There was another stable that had shipped in from Canada. I saw Billy VanWert at their barn, and asked him what he was doing there. He said that part of their horses, and all of their help, was going to ship to the VanWert farm in Goshen, Kentucky. I went by their barn several times a week, and started to get to know some of the help. One guy was always there. His name was John Rosenberg. John told me that he had fooled around a little bit with shoeing horses. He said that he had worked with jumping horses, and that he had rode some jumpers. I told John that he ought to go to work for me, but he said that his father didn't want him to shoe horses. He said that his family had a history of heart disease, and he thought the job would put too much strain on his heart. I told John if he ever changed his mind to let me know. John was from Maryland. He had a very good personality, and seemed like a good person.

It was almost unbelievable picking up all those new people to work for. I think that I had been looking for this all my life, but it would be nice to have some help. It would be at least a couple more years until my son, David, Jr., would be able to help me. I went to VanWert's farm one day, and was surprised when John said that he had decided to go to work for me, and be a blacksmith. Since I was getting so spread out with all the farm work and the race track work, I told John he could start doing some of the farm work now, and learn to do the race track shoeing slow and easy. Sometimes when people work without proper training they learn bad habits. I didn't know how much John knew about shoeing a horse, but I was sure that he would work out.

When we had to go to Ellis Park race track that summer, John could help me some at the race track in the morning, and then work at the farms in the afternoon. The next several months worked out good. My son, David, Jr., worked for Kenny Burkhart that summer at Ellis Park. That was good training for me. I had to teach myself how to regulate my work. Some of the horses that I was shoeing in the summer, would go to different race tracks in the winter. It would be hard to make all of this work out. I knew that I would lose some work, occasionally, because of connections, but that was just the way it would have to be. I wasn't a nervous person, but I was always anxious, and that made me aggressive. Maybe that was a good thing. I couldn't stand for someone to tell me that I couldn't do something.

That fall when we came back from Ellis Park, there were some new stables at Churchill. One of them was W. D. Lucas. I knew him from when he rode races for Doug Davis. He used to take me places, and out to eat. I wasn't shoeing his horses, because he had a blacksmith that worked for him, regularly, but I did go by this barn every day to say hello.

One day when I went by the barn, W. D. asked me if I would like to buy a nice, cheap, horse. I asked what the horse's name was, and he said "Happy Go On". I asked how much h e wanted for the horse, and he said that he wanted two thousand dollars. I told him that I would let him know something the next day. We only had a thousand dollars to spend, so I called my brother. He said that he would be at Churchill the next day, and we would buy the horse. I knew that I had seen the horse's name somewhere, then I remembered seeing a win picture of him, hanging on the wall, at the VanWert's farm. I had to go to the farm that afternoon, and when I walked in the office, there was a picture of Happy Go On, winning a big allowance race in Chicago the year before.

Mr. Lucas said that the horse was sound, but that he had some big ankles. I didn't say anything. The next day my brother didn't show up, and I didn't know what to do. I knew that he might be a nice horse, so I talked to Ray Frazer about it. Ray said that he had an owner who would buy the other half of the horse. I told Ray that I didn't want anyone fooling with the horse but me. He said that the man wouldn't bother me, and that he would let me use one of his stalls to put the horse in.

The next day Ray and I walked over to Mr. Lucas' barn. They knew each other from their riding days, when they were both jockeys. We bought the horse, and I led him back to Ray's barn.

He was such a good looking horse. It hadn't been long until he run. Bill told me that he bled in his last race, so he had put him on bleeder medication. That afternoon, I went to Dr. Harthill's office, and told him that I had bought the horse. He said that he would be by the barn in a little while and check him out. Dr. Harthill come, and run some blood test, and other different things. The next morning Dr. Harthill gave me the results of the tests. He said the horse was low on iron, and that he needed some T.L.C. After we started working on him, he seemed like a different horse. I really don't think he liked the groom that he had in the other stable. Some horses are like that.

John didn't know that I had bought the horse. The next morning when he got to work, I showed him the horse, and he was tickled to death to have a horse to fool with. The horse was seventeen hands tall, and John was a lot bigger man than I was, so he could lead him better than me. I got Frankie Adams to gallop him. Frankie and I had broke yearlings together at Hermitage Farm. Frankie had been a good jockey, but hadn't ridden a race in seven years.

Happy Go On was training super. We wanted to run him just to see what he would do. Mr. Frazer entered him in a race, and put one of the better jockeys on him. When John took him over to the paddock to run, the jockey took one look at his big ankles, and I knew the race was over before it ever started. When the horses broke out of the gates, the jockey pulled him straight up, and didn't let him run.

I was just sick. Now he would be put on the vet's list, and in order to get him off the list, we had to work the horse in front of the stewards. That was the last thing that Bill Lucas told me. He said that you couldn't get Happy to work in the mornings. We walked him in the barn for a couple of days, and I told Frankie what Bill said about the horse not working in the mornings. Frankie said that since I bought the horse, he seemed different. He said that Happy was an older horse, and they had probably been training him too hard.

We gave the horse a few days of easy training, and Mr. Frazer called the stewards, and told them we were ready to work him the next morning. I told Frankie to just do the best that he could with him. Frankie galloped Happy to the half mile pole, and broke him off. I knew the horse was rolling when the clocker yelled down and said that he worked in forty-eight and two fifths for the half mile. I could have fell over. I knew we had Mr. Happy Go On ready.

There was a race coming up in two days, for five thousand dollars. That is what he had been running for. I asked Frankie Adams if he would ride Happy, and he said, "Davie" I haven't rode a race in seven years. It's hard to ride after being off that long. He didn't even know if the stewards would give him a jockey license or not, at age sixty.

Frankie said that he would talk to the stewards, and if they would give him a license, he would ride Happy Go On. He came back in a little while with a frown on his face. I thought we were in bad luck, but he walked up to me and shook my hand. He said, "We are on". Ray wasn't sure about Frankie, because he didn't know him. When he entered the horse the next morning, he asked me who was going to ride him, and I told him, Frankie Adams. I told him that Frankie had gotten his license renewed that morning, and everyone was happy, because we knew that Frankie would get the horse to the winner's circle, if possible.

When race day come, John Rosenberg was going to take Happy over to the paddock. I didn't know what to expect, so I got a program. When I opened the program, I saw that Frankie was also riding a horse in the first race. John had shod another horse in the first race, and he said the horse that he shod would not get beat. Norma was there when John told me about the horse, but I never dreamed that she would bet.

When the first race was run, John and I were still at the barn, but Norma had already gone over to the races. As we walked around the track to the paddock with our horse, the tote board was lit up, and showed that the horse that John shod in the first race had won, and paid a big price. The horse that Frankie rode in that race had finished second by a nose. That made me even more nervous, because I thought that Frankie might be tired, now.

When we headed out of the paddock with Happy Go On, it was snowing so hard that you couldn't see anything. The ground was already white, and covered with snow. I thought that they might cancel the race, but I heard the announcer say "they are at the gate". The announcer couldn't see how to call the race until the horses turned for home, and he said, "I think it is Happy Go On" in the lead. When the horses passed the finish line, Happy Go On had won the race, and paid twenty six dollars to win. The double paid over three hundred dollars. I don't know how much John made on the race, but it was a lot, and one of Ray Frazier's grooms told me that Norma stuffed her purse full of money that she made on the race. She never did tell me how much money she made.

The next morning we sold our half of Happy Go On for five thousand dollars, and we got half of the purse. We really did good on that deal, but it was hard for us to have a horse for very long, because of our kids, and other obligations. John and I rode high for a few days, and I was tickled to death for Frankie Adams. He called us "Happy Go

On" every time he saw any of us. People on the race track talked about that deal for a long time.

Churchill always closes in the winter months. I was sure that we would have enough work at the training center, and at the farms to get through the winter. It was in the fall of nineteen seventy one, and Churchill was going to close for the rest of the winter. An empty race track was the most lonesome place on earth, considering that just a few months ago, there was one hundred and thirty thousand people there for the races.

I always enjoyed going to Mr. Van Wert's farm to work. I think everyone in the world knew him. My friend George Ogle would have his horses there this winter, and he was always good entertainment, by himself. There is one thing about horse people. There is never a dull moment. That is one reason I enjoy it so much. There is always someone wanting to buy you something to eat, or drink. Horsemen are a different breed of people.

John told me that he and his father went to Canada about this time every year, on vacation. He said that he would be gone for a week or so. It was almost Christmas, and there was several people who hadn't paid me for shoeing their horses. I was going to get on the warpath if someone didn't pay me. I made a few phone calls, and told the people that if that was the way they did business, not to call me any more to do their work. One of the Farms that I worked for had their office in Virginia. They hadn't paid me for five months. I called the office, and told the lady who answered the phone, that I would be

up there the next day, and that I wanted my money. She said that she would put my check in the mail right then. Two days later we got the check in the mail. I hated to be mean, but we had to live. I figured that some of the people would get mad, but it seemed like it got their attention. It also made me feel better.

Ray Frazer took a few horses to Turfway Park that winter. He had a blacksmith at that track, but he said that if the blacksmith got behind in shoeing the horses, that I could come and do a few horses for him. I did go to Turfway a couple of times, but it was very cold up there. The wind was always blowing fifty miles an hour and the horses would jump all over the place. The barns were all open, and I didn't like the place.

The barns that I worked in at home were all closed in, but in the winter time, the horses always seemed to be up tight. You really have to be careful, and not get hurt. I had gotten used to young and frisky horses at the farms, but some of the people on the race track are not used to them. After John and I started working together, I noticed that the horse John was working on, was always jumping around and being bad. Finally, one day, John told me that he got nervous when I was watching him work, and that made the horse nervous, too. After that, John would work on one side of the barn, and I would work on the other side. It always worked out well.

In early spring, the horses started moving back in to Churchill Downs. There was a big stable that moved in, and they had a whole barn full of horses. When I would walk through that area making my rounds every morning, I would always speak to the help. Once in a while, I would see a blacksmith there working. I found out the trainer was J. E. Morgan, and that he had a lot of good fillies. I just kept walking by their barn every morning, and speaking to everyone.

One morning when I walked by the barn, their foreman, Arthur, walked out of the barn toward me. He said that one of their good fillies was running in a race that day, and he wanted to know if I would shoe their horses. I told him that I would be happy to do their work. I said that I would be at the barn at ten o'clock. I went on to do my other horses that I had to shoe that day, and didn't think much more about it. I was just working in one barn over from them, and when ten o'clock came, Arthur came walking up the road.

I told Arthur that I was on my way to do the horse. When I got there they brought the filly out in the shedrow. Arthur told me that Mr. Morgan wanted me to grind all the toes off the shoes before I put them on her. I said OK, and went about my business, but under my breath I was thinking, "these people must be crazy". When I got finished shoeing her, I asked what her name was. He said her name was Brave Actress, and she was favorite in the stake race that day. When I left the barn I was thinking, "no way", but I was going to watch her run, anyway.

When you watched a race in those days, you had to go to the grandstand. When I got through working, I drove over to watch her run. After the race was over, I sat there in disbelief. Brave Actress had run one of the fastest seven eighth mile races ever run at Churchill Downs. I guess the joke was on me. I knew that I had learned a valuable lesson. I would not forget that I knew there was a reason for shoeing her that way. When I got in the right place, I would ask Mr. Morgan.

I went on working for Mr. Morgan. I knew that he had a lot of Ohio bred horses, and raced in Ohio all summer. He would come back to Churchill in the fall, on his way to Florida. Our working relationship lasted over twenty-five years.

The race track is like a big soap opry. John is starting to do good work, and my oldest son, David, Jr., is starting to carry some of my tools around for me at work. I think he is ready to put a shoe on now. It seemed like the Churchill meet didn't last long enough, but I also enjoyed working at Miles Park. That is part of working at the race track. You don't stay at one track very long. I always enjoyed the new people who came to Miles Park every year.

One of the people that I had been watching, and heard a lot about, was Ham Morris. Everyone said that he used to train dogs, but now he was training horses. One of his horses that I had heard about, drove a car. I had been working for Jimmy Lawson on Rose Island Road, who run a small horse operation. Jimmy told me that Ham wanted to know what days that I worked for him. While I was working, Jimmy walked over to Ham's barn, and told him that I was there. Ham said to tell me to come over to his barn when I was finished, and we could talk. I knew that Ham was a character as soon as I met him.

When I was finished with Jimmy's horses, I walked over to Ham's barn, and set up an appointment to shoe his horse, Butterscotch. While I was there, I saw the car that he drove. On the day that I was supposed to shoe Butterscotch, I brought Norma with me. I wanted her to see this, too. When we got to the barn, Ham told Butterscotch to turn the light on, and go out to the muck pit, and use the bathroom, and he did. I had never seen anything like that in my life. I only had to put shoes on his front feet, and trim him in the back. He was good to work on, just heavy, because he was a huge horse. Ham took him to shopping centers and he would drive the car. It was quite a show to see a horse drive a car. He was also on television several times. I worked on Butterscotch for a couple of years, until he quit driving the car.

Back at the race track I met another famous horse trainer. His name was Clarence Picou. I wasn't shoeing his horses, but I knew a lot of his help, and one of his owners. His owner's name was Fred Bradley. I knew that I would get to know Clarence better after he was around awhile. Race track people are a close knit group. Everybody knows everybody else's business.

I run in to Claudy Godsey one day, and he was telling me about one of his horses that had run down all of his life, and he was nine years old. I asked Claudy if I could see the horse. I thought that I might be able to shoe the horse, and make him stop hitting. Claudy said there was no way that I could stop the horse from hitting. I told Claudy that I bet him a hundred dollars that I could make him stop. We shook hands, and the next day I shod the horse. It was a few days before the horse run, and when he did run, Norma and I went over to the races to watch him. He won by many lengths.

We walked over to the test barn, and Claudy said that he had seen it, but he still didn't believe it. Even though the horse won the race,

Claudy was a little disappointed because the horse hadn't hit. Claudy pulled out a hundred dollar bill, and paid me. He run the horse several more times in his life, and he never did hit anymore. That was because of the good, early, training that I had gotten.

We were getting ready to move to Ellis Park again, and David, Jr. was going to help me this summer, and Norma was going to keep the other kids at home. I bought a nineteen thirty nine school bus for us to live in. We made a camper out of it, and put a stove, refrigerator, and an air conditioner in it. We parked it right beside Ray Frazier's barn. T. N. Snyder had two nice horses that Ray was training, and he wanted me to shoe them. John was going to stay around Louisville and the training center in Oldham County for the summer.

When all the horses got moved in to the track, I met a trainer from Arizona, his name was Carter Bond. He told me to stop by his barn in a few days. We always made rounds every morning, and if I had errands to run, I sent David, Jr. He already knew everybody on the race track. I noticed two local blacksmiths stopping at Carter Bond's barn every day, but I was stopping by his barn, too. That made me a little confused. I asked Carter if he knew the other blacksmiths, and he said that they had all been raised together. He told me that they were his friends, but he wouldn't let them shoe his horses. That made me feel very good.

I knew that someone had recommended me to him. Carter was a very private person, and I think that if you knew him for years, you still wouldn't know him at all. He would get me to shoe a horse whenever they run. He said that his wife worked in the Paramutials. I should have known to pay attention to his horses. He had a two year old horse that he started out running for thirty-five hundred dollars. Every time he run, Carter raised him up in price. One day I looked up when Keeneland was running, and the same horse was running in a hundred thousand dollar stake race. I opened up the paper the next morning, and the horse had won the race. Come to find out, the owner had paid forty thousand dollars for the horse, in the yearling sale, and Carter had run him for thirty five hundred.

I also met a man that summer that come from Aneta, Oklahoma. It was such a pleasure to know this man. He always had a lot of horses to train, and he was also a horse trader. He was a unique person, and his name was Boyd Finnell. I worked for him every year when he came to Ellis Park. The first time I met him, I shod the best horse he ever had, a horse named Air Boat.

David, Jr. and I were really enjoying Ellis Park this summer. One of Ray Frazer's owners would bring us steaks from home. They were home grown beef. We cooked out every night, and played horse shoes, and other games. Everyone brought tomatoes, cantaloupes, watermelons, and all the other things that were good to eat. It was like being in seventh heaven.

It was near the end of summer that Clarence Picou stopped me, and said that he and his blacksmith had had a falling out. He wanted to know if I could start shoeing his horses. I told Clarence that I could start doing his work after Ellis Park was over, but right now, I had all the work that I could do. Clarence said that he would make out someway until we got back to Churchill Downs.

When Ellis Park was finally over, everyone moved to all different places. That gave me a few days off, before I had to go to Churchill Downs. When I got to Churchill, there was a small stable that had moved in, that I didn't know. The trainer was Joe Marquette. His wife told me that Joe had a really good horse, that was turned out at Triple R. Farm. That is the farm that Blackie Huffman managed. The horse's name was Gallant Bob, and when they brought him in to the track, I couldn't believe what I saw. They had turned him out in the field without pulling his back shoes off, and he had jumped up and cut the quarter off of his front foot. It really looked bad.

Mr. Marquette doctored the horse's foot for several days. He and the vet got me to look at the foot, and see what I could do to cure the mistake that had been done. I told the vet that I would try to use some elasto plast, you put it in hot water, and form it to the horse's foot. Mr. Marquette said to try it, so we did. After I had finished working on the horse's foot, he walked away sound. If the procedure worked, the groom would apply reducine to the foot, every day, until the horse run in the race.

Gallant Bob seemed to be training good, but the foot looked bad, and horses' feet don't heal very quickly. They decided to go ahead and run the horse in a race. The day before he was going to run, I redid the elasto plast. The groom nearly had a fit. He said that Mr. Marquette was wasting his time to run the horse that way. I was a little worried, myself. I really didn't' know what might happen. When the horse run, he was in the feature race at Keeneland. I couldn't go to the races that day, so I had to wait until the next morning, and look at the results in the paper. I was afraid to open the paper and look, but when I did, I was pleasantly surprised.

The headlines in the paper read "Gallant Bob equals track record, in winning stake race". When I saw the groom, I told him that it was a good thing I put something on the horse's feet to hold him down. Gallant Bob went on to make a lot of money. The only bad part was that he was a gelding, and couldn't be used for a stud horse. I did Mr. Marquettes's blacksmith work for a couple of more years, until he stopped racing at Churchill Downs. He and his wife were very nice, and super smart horse people.

Norma told me that she was expecting again. The doctor told her that we really might have a Christmas present this time. Hopefully, everything will be OK. I was happy that I had picked up a lot of extra work, because we were definitely going to need the extra money, with another child on the way.

When Churchill Downs started its fall meet, I had a lot of horses to shoe. I had accumulated a lot of work in five years. I knew that John would be working on his own by the end of the year. I had started working for a small stable, run by a father and son team. Their names were Morris and Buddy Fife. The whole family was involved with the horses. They had three owners, and a couple of horses of their own.

One of their owners was Frank Weiger. He was a real character. He was always bringing something to the barn to eat or drink. When he first met me he started calling me "shoemaker". Some times people didn't know what he was talking about. He was always saying, "Hey shoemaker", "give me a winner". You don't see people like him anymore. I think that is why I liked this kind of work, because of all the different kind of people that you meet.

While Churchill Downs races was going on, we moved into a large house in LaGrange, Kentucky. The house was right in town, and had a small grocery store right across the street. The kids really enjoyed going to the grocery store. I bought a nineteen seventy two pick up for a work truck, and put beds in the back for the kids. I needed a new truck, because I would have to go to Turfway Park to work some this winter.

It seemed like time flew by while the races were going on. We were planning on having company for Thanksgiving. John, and some of his friends from Canada, were coming to our house for dinner. When everyone got together, our kids, and their kids, hit it off well. We all had a very nice Thanksgiving.

I didn't know if Norma would last until Christmas, before she had the baby. We always went to Lebanon, Kentucky for Christmas, to be with our families. Like always, the kids were anxious to go to grandmaw's house. We were all dressed and ready to go, when Norma said that maybe we should wait a minute. After a few minutes, she said that maybe I should take her to the hospital. The kids said to go on, that they would be OK. I took Norma to the hospital, and in just a few minutes, we had a Christmas Eve girl. We named her Tina Carol Wilson.

After Norma got back to her hospital room, she told me to take the other kids on to Lebanon for Christmas. She knew they would be disappointed if they didn't get to go. I went to the hospital on Monday, and picked Norma and the baby up, and took them home. Our older kids were old enough to help take care of the babies. That would help Norma a little bit, and they would have something to play with for a while.

I was going to take a little break during the holidays. Most of the horse action closed down during Christmas. When things opened back up, everyone wanted their horse shod first, as usual. I think horse trainers like to mess with people, but I have learned how to get even. They don't mess with me much, anymore. Some of the trainers wanted me to go to Turfway Park. That is the coldest place on earth in the winter. It was hard to work there, because it was so cold. They were supposed to build some new barns later on in the winter.

In the spring of nineteen seventy three, Bobby DeSinsi had a stable of horses at Turfway. One day he flagged me down, and told me that the state of Kentucky was starting an equine school for the back side help. He said the state would pay the people to learn to work with horses. He said that he had a friend, David Woods, who wanted to learn to be a blacksmith. He wanted to know if I might be able to help him. He said that David had been working for a trotting horse blacksmith, but wanted to work with thoroughbreds.

I told Bobby that I would like to meet David. We agreed to meet at the blacksmith shop at Churchill Downs, since the shop stayed open all year. I met David, and he seemed like a really good person. I knew that he had come from a good family, by the way he talked. He told me that he had applied for the state run program, and as soon as they OK'd him, he could go to work. I told him to call me when he was able to start working. I was going to have another apprentice. David and David, Jr. could learn together. They might be competitive after they got their business going.

David, Jr. was a lot further along at shoeing a horse than David Woods. He was at the point of tacking on shoes, but he was still in school. I was sure they would both work out OK. After David got used to me, he told me that his brother, Charlie Woods, wanted to be a jockey. I told David that I might be able to help him. I started asking around, and sent him to some people who would help him. He started getting on horses, got plenty of training, and it wasn't long before he was riding races. He rode really well for a long time.

David Woods was sharp after he really got into shoeing. I would try to trick him when we were working, but he would always catch what I was doing. He would say, "that's not the way you showed me how to do it". We got along well, and he would take me by his house once in a while. I met his parents, and they were certainly nice people.

Later on that spring, another trainer that we knew, Jess Futrell, came by the barn where I was working. He wanted to know if Norma was there. He said that he had a nice horse that he wanted to give her. He said that he had two horses, and one of them had broke his leg. He said that he was so disgusted, he just wanted to get out of the business. He said that he knew Norma would take care of the horse, and do a good job with her.

That night I told Norma what Jess had said. She said that if she took the horse, she would have to get a baby sitter. I told her that if she took the horse, she could help me some, too. She said, "that's what I am afraid of". The next day Norma went to Churchill to talk to Jess, and he gave her the horse. She had to get a stall, and all that worked out good. It gave us a place to hang out, eat lunch, and rest, if I needed to. The horse's name was Al's Princess. She looked like a stake horse. Norma was such a good care taker. I couldn't have been happier. Norma training horses, and two young men helping me work. Life couldn't have been better.

I was doing a lot of work, and was starting to work for a few top stables, with top horses. I knew it would take time, but I was getting good at correcting horses' feet, and it takes time for that kind of news to travel. I hadn't been working for Clarence Picou very long, and he had some horses that had foot problems. It wasn't long before I got the problems solved. It is amazing how much better a horse can run, when he is shod correctly.

It is amazing what you notice just by watching a horse walk by, or when they are galloping. Still, after all these years, I look at a horses' feet before I look at the horse. I used to bet the trainers that I could stop their shoeing problems, double or nothing. They have just about quit doing that, because it was costing them a lot of money. That was the best part of having sons that were blacksmiths. They already knew, what it took me a long time to learn. I know they won't give me any money back for teaching them.

When it got close to Derby time, everything got hectic. I had been working at Churchill Downs all day, and after I got home I ate dinner, and went to bed. In a few minutes, I got a phone call. The gentleman said that he was from A.B.C. Wide World of Sports, and wanted to know if he could do a story on me for the Derby. I told him that it would be OK, and he said that he would contact me. The next morning when I pulled up to the blacksmith shop, he knew who I was, and he was there to meet me.

He wanted me to go back out the gate, go back in the gate to the blacksmith shop, and go to the track kitchen to get coffee. They wanted to make bits of film on what I did in my regular day. I agreed to meet them at Kenny Burkhart's barn, after I made my rounds at nine thirty. The man told me that that would be fine. Mr. Burkhart had a seven year old horse that I thought would be perfect to shoe. After they got everything set up, they turned a big light on. The horse went crazy, and we like to never got him to settle down.

When we finally got the horse settled down, everything went well. They wanted me to show the public, the basic things about shoeing a horse. I knew there would be a lot of people watching the Derby news, because this was the year that Secretariate was running in the Derby, and that was all the people were talking about.

There was a big overflow of horses at Churchill Downs that year, so they opened Miles Park race track, early. I was trying to get enough time to go over there and check things out. The morning I went to Miles Park, I ran head on into L.C. and R.C. Hughes. They called L.C. Leonard, and R.C. Curley. Curley said that he had a mare that had been hitting, ever since she started running. She was running in a race at Churchill that day, and he wanted to know if I could shoe her, and stop her from hitting. He was kind of joking, but he said that his brother, Donald, had told them that I could stop her if anybody could. Curley told me the mare's name was Mito Wendy.

I started shoeing her, and she really didn't look that bad. When I was finished, I told Curley that we would just have to see how she run, and go from there. He said that he also wanted me to shoe the rest of his horses. I told Curley that since he was a Hughes, that I would have to. I had known Donald and Leonard for a long time.

When we got to a quitting point, I picked Norma up at the barn, and we went to the grandstand, and ate lunch. I wanted to be there when Mito Wendy run. She was in an early race, so we could go back to work after she run. When she run, it was hard to believe that she was the same horse I had worked on earlier. She broke out of the gate very quick, and stayed up near the lead. When the horses turned for home, she just pulled away from the rest of the field. After she won the race, I saw Curley down looking at her legs to see how much damage she had done.

I wasn't close enough to see what had happened, so Norma, David, and I went to the test barn, so that I could talk to Curley. When I walked in the test barn, I knew that Curley was pleased. He couldn't believe that she didn't hit at all. He said that Donald had told him that I was the only one he knew, that could stop her from hitting. I told Curley that the way the mare was made, she might not have a long racing career. Later on that summer, Mito Wendy won a stake race at Miles Park. That was what the owner was waiting for. It would make her babies worth a lot more money. Curley said that he had another good horse that I would be shoeing, but he was turned out at the farm, at the time.

The Fife's had claimed a cheap horse for two thousand dollars. The horse's feet was so sore, that he looked like he was walking on eggs. They wanted me to pull the horse's shoes off, and check his feet. I couldn't believe that a horse could run with his feet in the shape that his was in. His feet was blood red. The man they claimed the horse from had a walking machine, and the ground that the horses walked on was as hard as rock. Arnold James was Mr. Fife's owner, and I told him that there was no telling how good this horse would be, if I could get his feet straightened out.

They gave the horse a few weeks off to get his feet healthy. I put the shoes back on him, and the next time they run Duke of Zorn, they raised him up in price, to five thousand dollars. He won the race, easy, and as the summer went on, they just kept raising him up in price. Late in the

Ellis Park meet, they raised him to fifteen thousand dollars, and he won again. They didn't run Duke of Zorn anymore until Churchill Down's fall meet. They run him for twenty-five thousand, and somebody claimed him. Those are the things that make blacksmiths valuable. The horse started out running for two thousand dollars, and after I got his feet straightened out, he won for twenty-five thousand dollars.

Churchill was almost over, and Norma told me that she thought Al's Princess should run at Miles Park. The races there was four and a half furlongs. She said the filly needed to run in a race, even though she wasn't hardly ready to run, because she needed the experience. Norma had taken her trainer's test at Turfway Park, and passed it with flying colors.

When she entered Al's Princess in a race, she got in. The next day the stewards scratched her out of the race. They told Norma that her being a trainer was a conflict of interest, because I was a blacksmith. The stewards told Norma that she could run the horse in someone else's name, which is legal, but dishonest. Norma put Al's Princess in Kenny Burkhart's name as trainer, and Kenny let Norma use one of his stalls at the race track.

They entered Al's Princess again, and she run good. She came out of the race like nothing had even happened. We moved to Ellis Park a few days later. We rented a mobile home to live in just a few miles from the race track, and we really had a lot going on. Norma took care of the horse and the kids, and in a couple of weeks, Al's Princess was entered in another race.

On the day that Al's Princess was going to run, David Woods and I had to go to Frankfort, Kentucky and shoe some horses for Fred Bradley, who was one of Clarence Picou's owners. It was a long drive from Ellis Park to Frankfort, and we didn't get finished shoeing the horses until late afternoon. As we were driving back to Ellis, we were talking and fumbling with the radio. I found a station that was giving race results. I almost had a heart attack when I heard them say Al's Princess paid forty-one sixty. David and I looked at each other, and we were actually stunned. As we got closer to Ellis Park, we heard it again, on another station. By this time I was starting to feel like it was true. When we got back to Ellis Park, Norma told us that it was true. Everyone was really excited.

After everyone got settled down and back to work, Al's Princess acted like she had never run. I couldn't speak for everyone else, but that is what makes horse people want to go to work the next day. If you haven't had a horse to win, you can't imagine what it feels like. They had picked out another race for the filly. It was the same price race as the first one, just non-winner of two races. You might have to be a horse person to understand these conditions.

When race day come, Al's Princess was favorite in the program. Jockey Mike McDowell was riding her again, because he rode all of Kenny Burkhart's horses. When we got to the grandstand, the people weren't betting on her. She was in the second race, and I bought a ticket on her. I also wheeled all the horses in the first race with her in the second race. After the second race was over, Al's Princess had won again, and paid fifteen dollars to win. The daily double paid over three hundred dollars. After that, we started calling her "Big Al".

After she won her second race, a gentleman came by the barn one day, and said that Jess Futrell had bought Al's Princess from him, and that he had a fifteen hundred dollar lien against her that was supposed to be paid when she won. Norma didn't have any choice, but to pay him. The man was nice about it, and said that Al's Princess was a nice California bred horse, and that he wished us a lot of luck.

When they entered her the third time, I figured that it would be a tough race. I guess that it was, but Al's Princess was worth a lot more money than she had been running for. They entered her for non-winners of three races, for thirty-five hundred dollars. Mike McDowell told us not to worry, that she would win easy. She did win, and paid twelve dollars, even though she was favorite in the program, again.

After she won again, Kenny asked what we were going to do with her when the kids had to go home, and back to school. We told him that we really didn't know. Kenny told us that he would give us four thousand dollars for her, so we sold her to him, and was glad to get the money. Kenny was getting ready to ship the horses back to Turfway Park. It wasn't long before he run Al's Princess, again, for sixty-five hundred dollars. She won the race, and someone claimed her. We didn't see Al's Princess again until the next summer. She run in a stake race at River Downs Race Course, and won. I guess the owner wanted her for a broodmare, because I don't think she ever run again. With the money that Kenny gave us for Al's Princess, we bought some land, just outside LaGrange, Kentucky.

After all the horses moved from Ellis Park to Turfway, I didn't have very many stables there to shoe for. Curley and Leonard Hughes were there. They had started training for Eagle Mountain Farm, and had a really good stake horse. The horse's name was Village Dancer. They asked me if I would come to Florida Downs every month to do their work, since they always moved their horses to Florida when it got really cold at Turfway. I told Curley if I could get everything worked out, that I would do it. I didn't think that I would have very many horses to shoe at Turfway. Donald Hughes was going to stay, but he only had six horses at the time.

The last few winters at Turfway Park had been so cold that they had to cancel a lot of races. When the weather was so bad that they had to cancel the races, the trainers didn't shoe their horses, either. Clarence Picou was going to ship his horses to Hot Springs, Arkansas for the winter, and after David, Jr. got his blacksmith license, we might decide to go to Hot Springs for the winter, also.

The piece of property that we bought was the home place on a big farm. There was nothing there except the foundation of an old barn. I was interested in the garden spot. I knew that it would take a lot of work to clean the ground up, but after Churchill's fall meet, we would have some time to work on it. We had bought a new mobile home to live in, on the property, and if we liked the area, we would build a house.

All the time that Churchill races were running, it seemed like it rained every day. After the races were over, it sill kept on raining. Even though we had a little extra time, it was so wet that we didn't get much done that fall.

The first time I went to Florida for the Hughes brothers, Norma went with me. We drove straight through from Kentucky to Florida. I was completely worn out the whole week. I think it was due to us going from the cold weather, to the warm weather, so quickly. We got all the horses shod, and then we vacationed a little. We did some fishing at night off the pier, and we really enjoyed our working vacation.

In between the Florida trips, I bought a new, nineteen seventy-three twelve passenger van, that all the kids could ride in. I fixed a shop for me in the back, and up over my work section, I built a bed. That way, when we went somewhere, the kids could take a nap. After I got the truck fixed up, we went back to Turfway Park. The weather was just as bad as it was when we left. We went up there on race day, and mud was knee deep. I don't know how the horses run on the track with all that mud and water on it.

The next month when it was time to go back to Florida Downs, Norma and I decided to fly. I made a box that I could put all my blacksmith tools in, plus some extra horse shoes. It didn't take long to get to Tampa, which is where Florida Downs was. When we landed, we rented a car, and checked in with Curley and Leonard, at the race track. We talked for a while, and decided to start shoeing the horses the next morning.

After we got back down town, we rented a motel. We decided to just drive around for a while, looking through the orange groves, and checking out the fishing areas. The next day we shod several of their horses. Someone suggested that later on we all meet just outside the track at a little night club. All the race track crowd hung out there, and they had a country music band.

Norma and I ate early, and went to the club. As soon as we walked in, there were several people there who knew us. They also knew Norma from her singing at some clubs around Churchill Downs. Right away they told the owner that he should get Norma up on the stage to sing. He said that he would, but it would be a little while before the band started back playing. He told us to just lounge around for a while. It was just like being at home.

When the band started back playing, one of the band members come over to talk to Norma. He asked her what she was going to sing, and what key she wanted them to play it in. This might have been the funniest night that I have ever experienced. When Norma got up to sing, Curley hadn't gotten there yet. While she was singing, I saw Curley open the door and start into the club. Then he backed out, and closed the door. I really didn't know what he was doing.

When Curley finally came in the club, he said he thought that Norma had gotten drunk, and got on the stage, trying to sing. Then he remembered that Norma didn't drink, and she sounded too good to be drunk, anyway. Curley couldn't believe that Norma was a country music singer. We all really enjoyed that night.

The next day was not a good day. The horse that I was shoeing got crazy, and run backwards down the shedrow, and flipped over backwards on the car that we had rented. The first thing that I remembered, was that we had taken out extra insurance on the car, so what was done, was done. At least it didn't hurt the horse. That night we went down to the steel pier, and fished again. There is lights hanging down to the water, and you can see the fish swimming under the pier. It sure was a lot of fun.

The next day we only had a small amount of work to do. We were wanting to get home before dark. We were almost afraid to turn the car back in to the rental office. We told the lady at the office what had happened to the car, and she said "that ain't nothing. Last week an elephant sat on one of our cars."

When it was time to board the plane to go back home, I had a terrible feeling that something was wrong. I told Norma that we should get off the plane, but she said it was too late. We were already taxiing down the runway. We were on a non-stop flight from Florida to Louisville, Kentucky. After we were in the air, the pilot came on the radio, and said that we would have to land in Atlanta. He said that we had no brakes, and that the Louisville runway was too short to land the plane on. When we finally landed in Atlanta, we didn't have any trouble, although they had the foam truck on standby. We switched planes, and flew on to Louisville, Kentucky.

The next month, we had to go back to Florida one more time that winter. We didn't have any problems that time, but when you travel all over the country, time flies. It seemed like winter had just started, and it was almost over. The hardest part of going to Florida, was adjusting to the cold weather, again, when you got back to Kentucky. The next day, I had to go to Turfway to shoe all of Donald Hughes' horses, before he left there to go to Keeneland Race Track. Once you started working at Turfway, there was always someone wanting you to shoe a horse. Sometimes you just had to say no.

When spring came, and Hot Springs race meet was over, Clarence Picou came back to Churchill Downs with a barn full of good horses that he had accumulated over the winter. Clarence told me that he, and one of his owners, was looking at a farm in LaGrange, Kentucky. He said that the farm had an old Civil War house on it, and that sounded very exciting to me. He said that they hadn't closed the deal yet, but his owner, Mr. Jones, was a real estate agent, and owned some of the better horses that Clarence was training.

It wasn't but a few days until Clarence said that they had closed the deal. He wanted us to come out and check the place out. We went out on Saturday and Sunday, both. We did some looking around, and picked up some junk. We dug a hole in the ground, and made a place to cook out. Clarence brought a horse stall screen, and put it over the hole with the charcoal in it. We cooked on that almost every weekend.

What I really liked was some old, horse drawn tools, that we found at the farm. I told Clarence that it was a shame we didn't have some work horses to use out there. He had planned to bring some trail horses to the farm and leave them, so we could ride on the weekend. One of the trainers that I worked for at Churchill, had a lead pony. The pony was too crazy to pony horses with, but was a really good trail horse, and you could shoot a gun off him, so we bought him. He was a good pony for our older kids to fool with.

It wasn't very long until Clarence told me that he had bought two draft horses. We all enjoyed going to the farm. Clarence had a lot of friends who would come out on the weekend. We would cook out and ride the horses. I told David Woods, with a little of his help, I wanted to make a two horse sled. It took us a while to find the right kind of steel for the frame, and steel runners. There was a huge junk yard out by the fairgrounds, and we found a lot of things there that we could use.

I made all the steel parts in the forge, at Churchill Downs' blacksmith shop. It took us several weeks to make the sled, because we didn't have very much spare time. When we did get it finished, I found two truck seats that we bolted on to the steel frame. Then we had to work on making some harness for the horses. I knew all about making horse harness, because I was raised up with work horses, and had worked in the harness shop for Paul Ladd. One Sunday, after we got everything finished, we hooked the horses up, and it was really neat. A lot of people could ride on the sled, so when winter come, I was going to hook the horses to the sled, and take our kids to get a Christmas tree. I thought that would be a great experience.

The next week, at Churchill Downs, I ran into Larry Rue. He said that he had been looking for me, because Henry Forest wanted me to do their blacksmith work. Larry and I had galloped horses together at Clairborne Farm. Larry took me to their barn, and introduced me to Mr. Forest. He seemed like a really nice gentleman. He told me that he had a horse that might run in the Kentucky Derby, and that he wanted somebody to shoe the horse, that knew what they were doing. The horse's name was Kyber King. I told Mr. Forest that I would do my best. The next summer, Kyber King won the Travers Stake at Saratoga. I worked for Mr. Forest, shoeing his horses, until he quit training.

A few days later Jim Morgan asked me if I could come by his barn on Sunday. He said that he had a horse that had a problem. He said that he wanted the vet, the owners, and me, to get together and try to figure out what to do to the horse. That Sunday when I got there, the owners were already there. The vet was late, but did finally get there. Everyone discussed what to do with the horse. The vet said that they should give the horse away to a riding stable. He said that he had navicular problems, and he would never make it as a race horse.

After the vet left the barn, the owners asked me if I thought there was any chance that the horse might make it. I told them that I had been experimenting for a couple of years with that kind of problem, so they told Mr. Morgan that they would leave the horse there for three or four more months, and see what happened. I told the owners that it would take some time, and it would be pretty expensive.

The horse's name was Southwood Champ, and the first time I shod him, all the wedges that I put on his shoes, had to be make by hand, and the procedure took a lot of time. After he started training, he was going super. We were afraid to say anything. He had not trained for so long, it would take him thirty days to be ready to run, even if he stayed sound.

When Mr. Morgan got him ready to run, he said that he was going to run Southwood Champ at River Downs, because he was Ohio bred, and it would be an easier race. They entered him in a race, and the day that he had to ship and run, Mr. Morgan had me to check his shoes over good. When I saw Mr. Morgan the next day, he said it was no contest. Southwood Champ won the race, and they couldn't believe how well he came back. I watched him walk around the barn, and he was bouncing. I really felt good about him going so good.

Mr. Morgan said that there was a small stake race at River Downs that he was going to enter him in after Churchill was over. Mr. Morgan run the rest of the year in Ohio. When they run Southwood Champ in the stake race, he won again. In the next year, he made over a hundred thousand dollars. I thought that was pretty good, for a give away horse.

When we got back to Churchill Downs, Kenny Burkhart, who was one of my regular customers, informed me that morning, that I would like his new owner. He told me that Cawood Ledford had bought a couple of horses, and he was going to train them. I used to see Cawood walking around the barn area, but I didn't really know him. I think he liked Mr. Burkhart, because he was always clowning around. Norma and I had grown up on University of Kentucky basketball, and Cawood Ledford "was" Mr. University of Kentucky basketball. It was certainly a pleasure to know such a great gentleman.

One thing about the race tracks. You never get bored, because as soon as one race meet ends, you move on to another track. When we left Churchill Downs, we moved across town to Miles Park, where Clarence Picou had a whole barn full of horses. It was Picou horses everywhere. Clarence had some good owners, and they spent big bucks, on good horses. That's what it takes to do good at the races.

Clarence trained a horse for Fred Bradley named Voo Doo Vroom. When he was a two year old, he had a slab fracture in his knee. He was turned out at the farm for a couple of years. When they put him back in training, he had so much class, that when he run cheap, the other horses couldn't outrun him. During his racing career, he won about forty eight races. Clarence was leading trainer at the Miles Park race meet. Now it was time to move to Ellis Park.

It was unreal how good both of my helpers were doing. I think they will both be on their own this coming year. David, Jr. will be sixteen years old, and you can only teach them so much. If they have a lot of talent, they learn quickly, and they both had a lot of talent. I have been very lucky to have three smart people to teach.

When all the horses got moved in to Ellis Park, I ran in to my old friend, Carter Bond. He hadn't been to Ellis for a couple of years, but I still remembered some of the things he told me. He only had three horses, but you never knew what he was thinking. I knew that he didn't come all the way from Arizona for nothing. He said that they were just lounging around for the summer, and he would probably quit training after this year.

David at Churchill Downs 1974

Finally one day, he had a horse that was running. He said that he wanted me to come by the barn and check the horse's feet before he run. The horse was in the fourth race, and when I went by to check his feet, Carter asked me if I had any extra money. I told him that I didn't have much, and he said to go and borrow as much money as I could borrow, because the horse would not get beat. He had never told me anything like that before.

I left the barn, and tried to finish my work before the fourth race. When I got to the grandstand, and people saw me there, they knew that something was up. I sat with Donald Hughes' father-in-law, and I told him for what it was worth, Carter Bond had said that his horse wouldn't get beat. I told him it might, or might not, be true.

When the horses came on the track, the odds on Carter's horse kept flashing between six and eight to one. When the horses broke from the gate, Carter's horse was way back. It didn't look like he was going to do anything. He was twenty links from the lead, but when the jockey pulled this horse out in the middle of the track, turning for home, I have never seen anything like it. This horse looked like he had an extra motor. He made up all those lengths, and won the race by a length.

Carter run the horse for sixty-five hundred dollars, and someone claimed him. The next time, he run for twenty thousand dollars, and he won again. I guess Carter was trying to find out what kind of horse that he was. I didn't bet very much on the horse, myself, but to Donald Hughes' father-in-law, I was a hero for life. He always looked for that kind of horse to bet on.

When we went back to Churchill, most of the stables that I worked for, were going to stay there until the fall meet was over. When I was making my rounds, one morning, I went by Dr. Harthill's barn. He said that he had been looking for me, because he had a vet friend that was coming to Churchill to show me how to put acrylic in horses' feet. He was coming from Ohio State University. I told Dr. Harthill that I would be working at Triple R. Farm all afternoon, and he said that would be fine. He would call the other vet, and tell him.

As I went on making rounds, I saw another new stable that had shipped in to Churchill. Their colors were blue, white, and pink. They were in barn thirty-seven, and the barn was completely full of their horses. I figured they already had a blacksmith, because a stable that looked that good, should have a good blacksmith. I rode by their barn, and finally, on Sunday, I just had to stop.

When I talked to the foreman, he said that he thought nobody would ever stop. His name was Mr. James, and he said that they needed almost all of the horses shod. He said that the owner's name was W.L. Lofton. When I heard the name, I knew who they were. The trainer was Charlie Wonder, and Mr. Lofton was an oil man from Oklahoma. It was a super racing stable. I started shoeing all the horses, and one day Mr. James told me we had to pay special attention when we put shoes on one of the horses. He said the horse had one leg three quarters of an inch shorter than the others. I didn't have any problem with the horse, and if he run good, I guess I shod him right. It took me a couple of weeks to shoe all the horses, and Mr. James gave me Mr. Lofton's address. Norma made his bill out and sent it, and in three days, the check was back. It was like that every month, as long as I did the horses. Those kind of people is what made racing good.

Another stable that had come to Churchill with several horses, was Jim Mahoney. I knew Jim from when I first started working with the horses. He had worked for Eddie Anspach, when I did. One morning Jim asked me if I knew anyone who might want to buy a cheap horse for Turfway Park this winter. I told him that I would keep my eyes open. I went on making my rounds, and when I walked in to Mr. Fife's barn, one of his owners, Frank Weiger, was standing there. He said "shoemaker" do you know anybody who might have a cheap horse for sale that could run at Turfway Park this winter?

I told Mr. Weiger to come with me, and I took him over to Jim Mahoney's stable. I said, "Jim", this man and you are looking for the same thing. Mr. Weiger bought the horse. His name was Avispon. A few days later I went by Jim's barn, and he said that he had something for me. He handed me an envelope, and when I opened it up, it had two one hundred dollar bills in it. He said, "this is for finding me a buyer for my horse". The same day, I saw Mr. Weiger. He said, "shoemaker", I have something for you. He handed me two one hundred dollar bills. He said, "this is for finding me that horse". When Avispon started running that winter, and the next spring, he won five races. I felt very good about making that connection.

Thinking back on that race meet, I think the most colorful trainer that I met, was Dodge Fergerson. In his earlier years, he had been a mule trader. Dodge would buy four or five yearlings, cheap,

David working at Churchill Downs 1974

at the Keeneland fall sale, and the next summer, he would sell them for big bucks. He was really a good horseman. The only time he would let me shoe his horses, was if Norma was with me. He didn't want her to help me, he wanted her to sit there with him while I worked. He always brought her a box of candy, and they would sit and eat candy, while I worked. I couldn't win for losing. He always gave her the check.

Some of the years were more exciting than others. Most usually the horses generate the excitement, as a rule, and not the people. I had a small animal vet, that had horses. One of the horses was a nice stake horse, named Gee's Forward Thrust. The owner and trainer was T.N. Snyder. Gee's Forward Thrust had a problem. He was sore in his left front foot, and Dr. Snyder couldn't figure out why, and I couldn't tell him. He had the horse x-rayed and found nothing. He had him checked out by different vets, and they found nothing.

I told Dr. Snyder that we should talk, after he told me all the things that he had tried. I told him that there was only one other thing that I could think of. I said the horse might have a hidden quarter crack. Dr. Snyder jumped sky high. He told me that I was dumber than a box of rocks. That day when they took the horse to the race track to gallop, his quarter burst wide open. Right away, they called me over the loud speaker to come to barn ten. I got out of my car, and walked over to the barn where they were working on him. Dr. Snyder looked up at me, and never said a word. I laughed and said, "I can't believe that this dumb cluck blacksmith would be able to tell you something like that." Dr. Snyder said that he never would have thought about a quarter crack. He said he had learned a valuable lesson.

My work in Kentucky had gotten better in the last few years. When a lot of trainers leave Churchill Downs in the fall, now, they go to Turfway Park until after January, so that makes a lot more horses staying at Turfway than there used to be. We had finally gotten our mobile home moved to our property, and was in the process of building a small barn. I was glad that it was winter, so that we could get most of the work done around our place.

Next year would be a big year. It would be the One Hundredth Running of the Kentucky Derby. I was really looking forward to that. I was hoping that they would soon let horses stay in Churchill Downs for the winter. The only thing that is open at home in the winter, is the training center. I still had to go to Turfway Park some in the winter, to be able to keep shoeing the horses for the trainers, the next summer at Churchill.

I was always glad to get through the winter. Cold weather didn't agree with me, especially dark days. I didn't know where the time had gone. Our oldest son, David, Jr., would soon be sixteen years old. I guess time files, when you are having fun. The one thing that gets me through the winter, was planning our garden for the spring. The kids seem to really enjoy living in the country. We are going to have some chickens and pigs for meat, and a calf for beef.

It was finally spring, nineteen-seventy five. There was always new trainers who ship their horses in to run at Churchill Downs. The first week I run into Bill Mook. I had known him for several years. He was usually an assistant trainer for someone, and he usually had a couple of horses of his own. This spring he was working for Jim Eckroch. Bill told me that they had a lot of horses that was hitting, and that I had a lot of brain work to do.

The first time I did any shoeing for Mr. Eckroch, I didn't know much about him. He talked rough, but I didn't have to deal with him. Bill Mook gave me all the orders, and then he relayed the message to Mr. Eckroch. The first problem horse that I worked on was going to run in the classic, at Turfway Park, and Bill said that he hit real bad. I checked him out, and put some shoes on him. They galloped him a few days before they worked him, and he went super, and didn't hit. Bill had told Mr. Eckroch that he had never seen a horse that I couldn't stop from hitting.

The next day, Bill showed me a horse named Fast Irishman. He said that he didn't believe even I, could help him. I told Bill to let me know when the horse was going to the race track to work, because I wanted to watch him. Bill told me his work day, and I walked out to the race track to see if I could learn something.

After Fast Irishman came back to the barn from working, he had hit so bad that it looked like you had taken a hatchet and chopped the outside of his front leg, and chopped the inside of his back leg. I had figured out what he was doing, but I didn't know if I could change him enough to stop him from hitting. They were planning on running him the first day of the Churchill Downs spring meet, in the Derby Trial.

I told Bill to let the horse go, and let his feet grow as long as possible before we put the shoes on him. They had five days to let his feet grow, before the race. It took me a long time to shoe him. They were going to blow him out for the race, the next day. I was almost afraid to watch him work, but he looked like he was traveling good. When he come back to the barn, he hadn't hit. There was no blood anywhere on his legs. Mr. Eckroch was really pleased.

The next day I went on shoeing the rest of their horses. They had thirty horses, and Bill told me that I hadn't seen the worse one yet. When we finally got to him, Bill said that every good blacksmith in the country had tried to stop him from hitting, and couldn't. I was glad that Norma was with me that day, as a witness. I looked at the horse, and he seemed to be shod like a hitting horse should be. He had block heels on, and the inside block had been cut off. I remembered all those good blacksmiths trying to stop this horse from hitting.

I told Norma that I was going to do something unorthodox. I switched his back shoes from the way they had him shod. He was also going to run the first day of the Churchill meet. I thought it was kind of odd, that two of the worst hitting horses in their barn, would be running on the same day. When race day come, he was in an early race. He won the race, and didn't hit. When Fast Irishman run later, in the Derby Trial, he didn't hit either, and he won the race.

I really didn't know what to think. I knew that I had almost accomplished a miracle with those two horses. Fast Irishman went on to win several big races, and the other horse, a cheap claimer, won five races in a row. I went on to work for Mr. Eckroch for several years, and

I certainly enjoyed working for him. He always had several top horses in his stable.

That same spring, my friend, Oran Battles, shipped into Churchill with a barn full of stake horses. I think that Derby week, on the back side of Churchill Downs, is the most unique place on earth. I saw all kinds of famous people on the back side. Dale Robinson, who I always thought was a neat guy, came every year, and rode his horse around the barn area all week.

Howard Cosell was always around the race track at Derby time. I had made David, Jr. a little blacksmith apron when he was very young, and he started carrying my blacksmith tools around, and helping me. Howard thought that was the neatest thing he had ever seen. He was always coming around the barns and telling us stories. I just loved it. The day before the hundredth Derby, I had to do a lot of work, because I was shoeing a lot of horses that was running on Derby day.

I shod a horse for Clarence Picou, that was running in the daily double, I did one that was running in the big stake race, and two horses in the Twin Spires. There was so many horses entered in the Twin Spires that year, that they split the race. Oran Battles had a horse in each of the Twin Spires races, and I had shod both of them.

I never worked on Derby day. There was always lots of parties on the backside on Derby day, and you could eat and drink almost everywhere you went. Our kids always went with us that day, and they really enjoyed it. I always started nipping, early. We always eat all morning, and talked to hundreds of people. Everyone knew everyone, on the backside of Churchill Downs.

When it got close to race time, Norma and I decided to walk over to the race track and get a daily double ticket. Someone had given us a horse to bet in the double, with the horse that I had shod for Clarence the day before. There was so many people in the grandstand that you could hardly move. Both of the horses we bet on in the double, won, and the daily double paid over two hundred dollars.

After the second race run, Norma said that she was going back to the barn area. I told her to leave me some money, and she left me a twenty dollar bill. There I stood, in the middle of one hundred and forty thousand people, with twenty dollars, and no beer money. I thought Norma was being mean to me, but actually, she got my adrenaline going. I bet on the next couple of races, and cashed both tickets, and then I had some beer money. I bet some more on the next couple of races, and both of them won. Now I had quite a bit of money.

When Oran Battles' horse run in the first half of the Twin Spires, he won and paid thirty some dollars. Now I had enough money to buy Churchill Downs. I thought after every race that my luck would run out, but Mr. Battles' other horse run, in the second half of the Twin Spires, and he won, too, and paid almost thirty dollars. If I hadn't had a few beers, I would have gotten really nervous.

When the Derby race come up, Dr. Harthill told me that Canonade would win the Derby. When it was time to bet, I bet five hundred dollars on Canonade, and then I got nervous. There was so many people you couldn't enjoy yourself, but I was sure trying. I couldn't see the race, and I could barely hear, but I could hear enough to know that Canonade won the Derby. I went to the ticket window, and there was already a long line. Canonade was favorite, but he still paid a little over five dollars to win.

After I cashed my ticket, I headed back across to the backside. As I started around the track, I was having a hard time walking. It felt like I was top-heavy. A gentleman named Slim, who worked on the backside, came along and took my arm, and helped me along. After we got around the track, I went toward the track kitchen, and Slim went in the other direction. I gave Slim some money for helping me. I guess I was giving money to everybody. One of the trainers that knew us, went and told Norma that she had better come and get me. He said that I had money coming out of every pocket, and that I was giving it to everyone I saw. After Norma showed up, I knew that my adrenaline would settle down. If I live to be two hundred, I will never forget the One Hundredth Kentucky Derby. I wish I had some way to freeze that day, and frame it. It takes a few days to settle down after each Derby, but it is worth anything that happens, just to experience the day.

A few days later, my friend George Ogle, came by the barn where I was working, and asked me if I would do him a big favor. George said that he was a friend of Diane Crump, and that she had a horse that had a hitting problem. He said that the horse was a nice two year old, and that she wanted me to shoe her other horses, also. I told George that I would stop and see Mrs. Crump as soon as I could.

When I finally got by her barn, Mrs. Crump showed me her problem horse. He seemed like a nice horse, and was well broke, but he had a really bad hitting problem. I told Mrs. Crump that sometimes I had to shoe a horse twice, but I could usually stop the horse from hitting. When I started shoeing her horses, Mrs. Crump told me that she was the boss, not her husband. Everything worked out well at her barn. I should have paid George Ogle for being my agent. George sent me a lot of work over the years.

The horse of Mrs. Crump that was hitting, was going to run at Churchill on Saturday. Norma and I had already planned to take the kids to the races on Saturday. There was a big stake race that day for two year olds. I had only heard Diane's horse's name once, when I shod him. Golden Chance Farm had an even money favorite in the stake race, and I had just started shoeing horses for them. When the race was run, I sat there in disbelief. Diane's horse won the race, and paid sixty some dollars to win. I knew he hadn't hit, and Diane told me if he didn't hit, he would win. I just didn't listen.

I went on to work for Diane Crump for almost three years, until they quit racing at Churchill Downs, but Golden Chance Farm was one of my biggest stables that I worked for. They had forty head of horses everywhere they went. Smiley Adams, the stable foreman, and I only had one little spat. One afternoon we were working at his barn, and my son, David, Jr., was finishing feet for me. When Smiley come in the barn, he told me he didn't want a green horn working on his horses' feet. I said OK. That fall, when they sent forty horses to Turfway Park, and I couldn't shoe all the horses, who do you think got the job? My son, David, Jr. I had been around long enough to realize that horse trainers have bad days, too. They are only human.

As the Churchill meet came to a close, most of the horses moved across town to Miles Park. They were leaving Churchill's barn area open this summer, and there was a lot of horses staying there as long as they could. Most of the stables at Miles Park came there every year. I was starting to not like Miles Park very much, because every morning when we got there, everything was covered with a white coat of chemicals, that was coming from a chemical plant in the area. It couldn't be healthy, but everyone made it through the year, every year. I was always glad to get away from Miles Park.

After we left Miles Park, and went to Ellis Park, something awful happened. Donald Hughes had a barn half full of horses, and some of the other people that I worked for had horses in that barn, too. David, Jr., and I were planning to start shoeing Donald's horses the next week. I was going home that weekend, and David, Jr. was staying at Ellis in case some of our clients needed something done. He was going to shoe Donald's pony while I was gone.

I got home, and the next morning when I looked at the paper, I couldn't believe what I saw. On the front page of the paper it showed the barn with Donald's horses in it,

David working at Churchill Downs 1974

had burned down. They were only able to save a couple of horses, and everything else, including everyone's equipment, was gone in the fire. It was a terrible sight. It takes trainers a long time to recover from something like that. It took a couple of weeks to find out who started the fire. Some guy from Ohio had started the fire.

One good thing that happened that summer, our son David, Jr. turned sixteen, on July the eighth, and that was the day that he got his blacksmith license. He was one of the youngest to ever be licensed as a blacksmith in Kentucky. It scared me to watch him work so easy, to be so young. He was a very talented young man.

There was another man who I met at Ellis Park that summer. He started out with one horse, and over the summer, he wound up with twenty. His name was James Arnett, and his daughter, Karen, was his assistant trainer. They won a lot of races that summer. The family stables seem to do well in the horse business. Everyone at the race track asks me every fall if I am going to Hot Spring, Arkansas for the winter. I had been thinking about that. Maybe we will go when David, Jr. gets a little more experienced.

Just before we left Ellis Park, I met an older gentleman, who introduced himself as Judge Partee. He wanted to know if I could come to his farm in southern Illinois. He said that he had twelve horses that needed to be shod. We planned a time to go, as it was about a hundred miles from Ellis Park.

The farm was hard to find, and when I drove down the lane, you couldn't see the barn, for the weeds. They had burlap sacks sewn together to put over the horses to keep the flies off of the horses. When they led the first horse out to shoe, he was a huge, good looking horse. He stood fairly good, and as they kept bringing each horse out, they all looked exactly the same. I had never seen anything like it. I shod twelve horses, they were all studs, same color, same markings, and same weight. When we got finished shoeing the horses, Judge Partee told me to come up to his office, and he would give me a check. It was a good day financially, but I earned every nickel of it. It was a good thing Norma come along to help me.

When Ellis Park closed, I was hoping to slow down some this winter. We had some hogs and a beef to kill. Our kids seemed to like our little farm. We had grown a beautiful garden that summer, and everybody had jobs. Everything had worked out good, but it was hard to figure out the horse business. You never knew who was coming to a race meeting. Some of the trainers change directions from one year to the next. You have to be careful not to get overloaded, because that is worse than not having enough work. There are several of the people who I work for that does go to Hot Springs in the winter, and they would like to have the same blacksmith the year around.

Eventually, I might get my work to the point, that I could go to Hot Springs, but a couple of our kids were still too young to leave all winter. Most horse people's life is just about the horses, but the ones who have families, have to put them first. That is what I loved most about my wife. She always took care of all of us.

As the winter drew to an end, Churchill Downs opened again, and the horses could move back there. I met another trainer who had started out small, but now is getting some nice horse. The trainer was Jim Padgett. He was such a nice guy, and good horseman. There was also a trainer from Lexington, Kentucky, who was at Churchill. His name was T. McCan. He had some good owners, and they were buying some nice horses. He was also going to Hot Springs in the winter. David, Jr. and I had been talking about going to Hot Springs in the winter of nineteen seventy-eight. There was a lot of trainers going there for the winter, instead of going to Turfway Park. We had tried to tie all the loose ends together, so that we could go to Hot springs this winter.

When we were ready to go, I really didn't know what to expect. Some people told me they liked Hot Springs, and some people didn't. If everything worked out, we would be OK. We actually went a little early. The races didn't start until February, but we had some work already there.

When we got to Hot Springs, we drove around a little bit, then went to the race track. I saw a boy that I knew, and he told me about a place on lake Hamilton. We drove out to the lake, and found the place. It was not fancy, but the apartment was big enough for two people. Barb was the lady who owned the place, and she seemed to be very nice. The place seemed to fit our budget, and there was a little restaurant out in front. The motel was about four miles from the track, and I thought it would work out fine.

We rented the apartment, and unloaded the car. We were really tired from driving. The next morning we went to the track to check things out. There wasn't very many of the horses that we worked on there, yet, so that gave us some time to find out where everything was.

When the horses started moving in to the race track, they come pretty fast. The only thing that bothered me, was that I had to take a blacksmith test in Arkansas before they would let me work. They waited until the races started before they gave the test. If I failed, it would be thirty days before I could take it again. By then, all my work would be gone. I had heard some bad things about this test.

When the day come to take the test, everything went well. They told me to make a bar shoe. After I made the shoe, the man who gave me the test, took a hammer and beat the shoe wrong side out. Then he said I had failed the test. The next morning, all the trainers that I worked for, went to the Arkansas Racing Commission. They asked them what was going on. I had worked for some of the best stables at Churchill Downs, and I was good enough there, so why wasn't I good enough in Arkansas. They said that they would give me another test that day. I took the test, and in about thirty minutes I had my blacksmith license.

I also got another surprise that day. Don Combs, the trainer of Dust Commander, asked me if I would shoe his horses. I had galloped Dust Commander's sire, Bold Commander, when I worked for Mr. Fitzsimmons, years before that. It sure is a small world. Mr. Combs had a barn full of good horses. I had so many horses to shoe down there, I couldn't find them all. One of the good parts about being down there, was that David, Jr. knew everybody on the backside.

Just a few days after we got there, Barb, the lady at the motel, needed some wood for her stove. She heated the restaurant with it, and she didn't have any way to get wood. David, Jr. and I were used to cutting wood, so I told her if she would show us where to cut it, we would cut her all the wood that she needed. She said that her brother had a farm just up the road, so we went to the farm on Saturday and cut two truckloads of wood. I guess that David, Jr. and I got some extra feathers in our cap.

A few days later, the weather forecast was calling for a lot of sleet and ice. That was just what we didn't need. We did get it, and there was so much ice, you couldn't go anywhere. The races had to be called off for a few days, and when the races were called off, the trainers didn't shoe any horses, and then we got behind. That's the way it always happens. One of the trainers we worked for, Forest Kaelin, had thirty horses. My friend, James Mahoney, quit training, and went to work for Forest as his assistant Trainer. The weather was a factor for awhile, but when it did break, we got really busy.

One of the trainers, T. McCan, told me he thought he might have a derby horse, and he wanted me to check on him, regularly. The horse's name was Special Honor. T. McCan was a very nervous man. There was a barn outside the back gate that had about twenty stalls in it. Joe King was stabled in that barn. I would check on Mr. McCan's stable, and then if I needed a break, I would walk back to Joe's barn, and talk to him or his help. They knew what I was doing, and they always had coffee and doughnuts. Joe was Forest's son-in-law, and I had to shoe something for Forest and Don Combs every day, because they both had so many horses. James Burchell had a farm just outside of Hot Springs, and he had two sons the same age as David, Jr., so that gave him somebody to run around with.

One day I made a big mistake. I was working on a horse for Mitch Shirota. Every time I worked in his barn, I would hear things that told me they were getting ready to cash a ticket on the horse. The day the horse was running, I walked over to the races to watch him run. I didn't have any money with me, but all of a sudden, bells started ringing in my head. I saw Joe King, and I asked him if I could borrow two hundred dollars to bet on a horse. He said OK.

While I was waiting for the horse to run, I saw a friend of mine from home. He asked me what I was doing at the races. I told him that I was going to bet on Mitch Shirota's horse. He asked me if I would bet on the horse for him, because he had to go somewhere before the race run, but he would be back, When it come time for me to bet, I just couldn't do it. If the horse got beat, Joe would take the two hundred dollars out of my check, so I didn't bet for me. The horse won, and paid forty-one dollars. I was sick. When my friend come back, I gave him the ticket that I had bet for him. He couldn't believe he had bet two hundred dollars on a horse that paid forty-one dollars. He cashed his ticket, and handed me three one hundred dollar bills. That made it a little bit easier for me, and he was tickled to death. The next morning, I gave Joe back his two hundred dollars. He always thought that I bet.

The trainer that I really started paying attention to was Don Combs. He run in two filly races, one on each weekend, and won them both. I knew he had some good fillies and mares. There was a lot of money for the female horses at Hot Springs. There was a lot of purse money for the other horses, too, and T. McCan was getting Special Honor ready to run in a big race.

I didn't think that Mr. McCan ever went to bed. He was so nervous that he just walked up and down the shedrow, day and night. He was so nervous that he made the horses nervous, too. The closer to the horse running, the more I went by the barn to check on him. It made Mr. McCan feel better. When the day come for Special Honor to run, I wanted to go over and watch the race.

When the race started, Special Honor broke in front. The jockey had so much hold on him, he started throwing his head up and down, and after he run about three quarters of a mile, he just stopped running. I knew that Mr. McCan was really disappointed, even though he didn't say much. I kept going by the barn every day, trying to cheer him up. I knew that he would be alright, but sometimes the owners are the ones who raise cane. Anyway, I had to think about a lot of other trainers. There was several horses that had to be shod, every day.

I think this is the first time since I started working as a blacksmith, that I didn't have a lot of problem horses to work on. I started my day at Winston Neal's barn, where they had jelly donuts every morning. I could sit there for awhile, and have coffee and donuts, and a lot of the trainers that I worked for, would come by and talk for a few minutes. I didn't think about it then, but that was a good way to see everybody, without going anywhere.

Then I would go to Jim Padgett's stable. Jim was a class act. He had a derby horse the year before, but he never got excited about anything. He always knew how to talk to you. I really enjoyed working for those kind of people. All of the trainers that I worked for was winning races, and when they did good, it made me do good.

I have kind of enjoyed being at Hot Springs, but there was something that I just didn't trust about the place for some reason. I really didn't know why. My son, David, Jr., said that he would never come back here, but my brother come to the races several times during the winter. He really enjoyed coming to Hot Springs, Arkansas. I guess the reason I didn't like it, was the way they treated me on my blacksmith test. The best part was, it was starting to be good weather at the end of the race meet, and all the big races had started running. I was glad to be working for Don Combs, because I think he has won all the filly races he run in. He doesn't take his horses to Churchill Downs in the spring, but he certainly had been heard of at Hot Springs.

Before we left Hot Springs, Special Honor was going to run again. I had been going through the same routine of going by and checking on him every day. The day he run, I went over to the races, and watched him run, again. He run the same identical race that he run the first time. The next day I was working at Forest Kaelin's barn, and we were talking about Special Honor.

I told Forest that I knew the rider didn't fit the horse, and I thought Mr. McCan should switch riders. I never thought any more about it, but sometime between Hot Springs and Churchill Downs, Forest told Mr. McCan what I had said. When we got to Churchill, every time I pulled up to Mr. McCan's barn, he would get in his car and leave. He hadn't spoken to me since we got back from Hot Springs. When he had a horse for me to shoe, he would just write the horse on the blacksmith board in the barn. I thought if Mr. McCan could play games, I could play, too.

Mr. McCan didn't run Special Honor until the Derby. He run terrible. It almost seemed like he wasn't a grade one horse, after all. I knew that everyone around the barn was unhappy. Every day when I went by the barn, I didn't say much. I just did my work. A few weeks later, I was looking in the paper at the entries for the Ohio Derby, and Special Honor had been entered, with a different jockey riding him.

I didn't get to watch the race that day, but I will never forget the headlines in the paper the next day. "Bobby Breem rides Special Honor to Victory in the Ohio Derby, and pays Two Hundred and Twelve dollars to Win". I felt like the hero, and I didn't even do anything. I just made a statement. The next day when Mr. McCan and Special Honor got back to Churchill, Mr. McCan was very happy. Thistle Downs had given the winning trainer, T. McCan, a watch for winning the race, and Mr. McCan wanted me to have it. What he did that day got inside my heart. I accepted the watch, and wore it for many years.

When more stables started moving in to Churchill, I got another surprise. Ted McClaine, whom I had worked with at Clairborne Farm when he was a groom, was now training the Clairborne Farm horses. It sure was a small world. I never dreamed about Ted training horses. It seems like half the people I work for now, I worked with, in the earlier years of my life. It wasn't planned that way, but it tells me if you try to do right, things do better.

Another stable that moved in to Churchill that year, was Crimson King Farm. They always had at least thirty horses at the track. Crimson King was a big farm in Lexington, Kentucky. Their foreman asked me if I would shoe their horses. I had spent my whole life getting to this point. Between me, my son, and the other two blacksmiths that I had gotten started, we were working for all the big stables at Churchill Downs. To top it all off, Harry Trosik's blacksmith went to Chicago, and Mr. Trosik wanted me to do his work. It would only be for three weeks, but he had forty horses. That's a lot of work to pick up in your spare time, but I told him that I would try.

A few barns down from Crimson King Farm stable, I ran in to my old friend, Bill Mook. He told me that he was getting ready to go to work for Jack VanBerg. He said that Jack was building a huge training center out at Sky Light, Kentucky. Bill said that it would be something for me to think about. Bill still had a couple of his own horses at the race track. I guess I should pay Bill to be my agent.

It was nice to be back at Churchill Downs, and close to home. My wife and I had started taking our kids to church at Eighteen Mile Baptist Church. It was a small church in the country, like the one we had gone to as kids. It was one of the oldest churches in the county. We had been going to the church for several months when our pastor, Brother Berry, told us that he had inherited a church bell. He wanted the church members to donate enough money to build a steeple to put the bell in. For some reason, the congregation didn't seem to want a steeple on the church. I guess they thought it might not look right on a two hundred year old church.

I thought about it for a few weeks, and I told Norma that I wanted to build the steeple, and donate it to the church. I think Norma thought I was crazy, but when I told Brother Berry, he was tickled to death. I told Norma that she would have to help me, and I promised her there would be no bad language. This was for the church. We went to work on the steeple, and even though I wasn't a carpenter, there was a lot of things that I could do. I drew me a blueprint in my mind, and we started cutting from the lumber that I had stored in my barn. I built the steeple in two sections. I guess it took the better part of a month to build.

When I took the steeple to the church, I was going to put it together, and run a chain through the middle of it so a crane could lift it up on the church. I went up to Barrickman's garage, where I hung out a lot, and Mr. Barrickman asked me what I was doing. I told him that he probably wouldn't' believe me if I told him. Right away he asked me what I was going to do about putting a cross on top of the steeple. I told him that was why I had come to see him. He said he would make a stainless steel cross, and donate it to the church. I never thought anything so tough to do, could turn out so easy.

When we got the steeple to the church, we put it together. I put a chain up through it, with a hook on it. One of the men at the church said that somebody with a crane was coming through that area in a couple of days, and had donated their services to put the steeple on top of the church. Now I had to worry for two days as to whether it would fit, or not. When they did come and put the steeple up on the church, it fit like a glove. They took the chain out, and put the cross on. That was thirty years ago, and it still looks good. I think that was the proudest moment of my life. In the weeks and months that followed, it seemed like my whole life had changed. I can not explain how I felt inside. I know the Lord works in mysterious ways, and I have had nothing but good luck for the past thirty years.

A few months after we made the steeple, I saw Bill Mook, and he asked me if I was ready to go to work, shoeing horses, for Jack VanBerg. He told me that Jack was going to have a big operation, and that I should think about going to work there. Bill said that I could work at the training center every afternoon, and that Jack always had at least forty horses at the race track to shoe. He also said that Jack raced at all the Kentucky tracks. This job would be hard to turn down, because it was so close to home.

I had worked on a horse for Jack a couple of years before, that was trying to founder. Dr. Harthill had gotten me to shoe the horse. He told Jack that I knew how to use acrylic, and aluminum pads on this horse. The horse responded very well, and although he would never be able to run again, he wound up being one of the best broodmare studs, ever. I knew it would be good to be in this position. Jack VanBerg had a reputation world wide, and it would be an honor for me to work for a man of that caliber.

Eighteen Mile Creek Baptist Church

By now, my youngest son, Daniel, was already going to work with me. It wouldn't be long before he would be shoeing horses, too. He already knew every horse on earth. We all talked about the job at VanBerg training center that night, and it really sounded good. I had heard that Jack tried to intimidate people, but I thought that I might be as sharp as Jack, and I never forget that.

As the months went by, it was a big operation. It took a couple of years to learn all the broodmares, but after about three crops of horses, you get familiar with them. You remember them as babies, then yearlings, and then two year olds. By then, you knew most of the horses. The racing horses were done by numbers. Jack had ninety-eight stalls in the training barn, and the number of horses on the whole farm was close to four hundred.

After a couple of years at the training center, I was shoeing so many horses every month, that my bill was getting complicated, so Jack wanted me to leave him a bill at the office every Monday morning, and when I got back from the race track, my check would be in my mail box at the office. That is the way he paid me for fourteen years, every week. It was one of the best jobs in the country. Just to make myself feel better, I kept a separate record book on all the horses that I shod for Jack. I kept it in a wall box right beside where I worked every day. Every time I knew that Jack was coming to town, I would go through my book to jog my memory. There was several times over the years, when Jack would ask me about a horse, I could give him the answer right off the top of my head. I knew Jack wondered how I could do that. In all the years I worked for Jack, I tried to stay in front of his thinking. I think that is why we got along so well. I not only liked to work for him, I liked Jack as a person.

After people found out that I was working for Jack, a lot of them wanted to know if I would work for them. It was nice to have that happen, even though I couldn't shoe all of their horses. There was a lot of stables that would be shipping their horses across the country, and they would stop at the training center for a day or two. There was several small stables that would stay there for several months. Most of them were people who had worked for Jack. I never saw a man who had so many friends. The training center was central headquarters, and sometimes I would shoe five or six horses one day, and the next day they would be gone. It took me forever to realize that the horses I was shoeing every day, was being shipped out that night to another location.

Some of the most memorable times that I had while I was working for Jack, was at Derby time. Jack threw a huge Derby party every year, and there was hundreds of people who come to the training center all during Derby week. One of the big highlights was that Jack and Bob Wright had bought a four horse hitch of Hackney horses, and a big coach. Jack would bring the horses and coach over to the training center during Derby week, and ride the visitors all around the farm. Bob Wright kept the horses at his farm, in PeWee Valley, and I would go over there every month and shoe them.

My youngest son, Daniel, was starting to do a lot of work. It wouldn't be long until he would be out of school. Jack was in town one day, and he asked me to go over to the lay-up barn, and trim a couple of horses. He said that I could buy one of the horses cheap. I asked him how much he wanted for the horse, and he said twenty-five hundred dollars. The horse was a three year old that had never run, because he had some problems. Right away, Daniel wanted to buy him. I told Jack that I would buy the horse under one condition. That I could keep the horse there, until he was ready to run. Jack said that I could keep him there, so I thought maybe it was time to get in to the business. Our kids were pretty much grown, and I enjoyed going to the races with Daniel. He was like a racing form.

One day while I was working at the training center, Ernie Retamosa came by and wanted to know if my oldest son, David, Jr., and I, could go to Ocala, Florida, and shoe some horses for him. He said he had fifteen horses at a farm in Ocala, and wanted to know if we would make the trip over the weekend. I told him we would, and after we finished work on Friday afternoon, we headed out to Florida.

When we got to Ocala, it was late afternoon, so we got a motel room. Someone had told me that Eddie Anspach, the man who I had started out with as a teenager, was running a farm in Ocala. I got the phone book, and looked up his number. I dialed the number and Mr. Anspach answered. He sounded just like he had when I was young. Mr. Eddie was eighty-three years old. It had been twenty-five years since I had talked to him. He was really glad to hear from me.

David working at Churchill Downs in 1974

After I talked with Mr. Eddie for a while, David, Jr. and I went to a fish place to eat. When we walked in to the restaurant, we saw several horse pictures hanging on the wall. David, Jr. was in several of the pictures. A good friend of David, Jr.'s owned Rita Maria, and he had run her for them the day she won the race. It was odd to drive all that distance, and walk into a restaurant, and see a bunch of your own pictures hanging on the wall.

When we got back to Kentucky, we went to the training center to work. Jack was there, and he had bought six yearlings out of the yearling sales. The next morning they took the yearlings to the broodmare barn. Jack wanted me to go over and look at the yearlings with him. Jack showed me the horses, and said, this one here, Alysheba, will win the Derby. Not only did he tell me that, I think he told everybody that looked at the yearlings, the same thing, so everybody just planned on Alysheba winning the Derby.

Those yearlings were broke at VanBerg's training center that fall, and Jack sent Alysheba to California for the next several months. I didn't see him again until the fall of nineteen-eighty-six at Turfway Park, the day he run, and broke his maiden. I had to shoe him when he shipped in. He didn't have any back shoes on. It wasn't long after Alysheba broke his maiden, that Jack sent him back to California. I didn't see him any more until a little while before the Derby, and the rest is history.

Alysheba did go on to win the Kentucky Derby, the Preakness, the Woodward Handicap, and the Breeder's Cup Classic, along with numerous other races. He was the highest money winner of all times, at that point in his career.

One day while I was shoeing a horse at the training center, a boy that lived down the road came by the barn and asked if I would teach him to be a blacksmith. He said that he didn't want to learn to shoe horses, just to trim them. The boy's name was Greg Hardin. I told Greg that you couldn't teach the trade without teaching the whole thing. People who have horses to trim, also have horses to shoe. Greg started helping me, and he did pretty well. After Greg worked with me for a couple of years, he got married, and he said he thought he could make it on his own. By this time Daniel was almost ready to work on his own. I had been very fortunate to have the opportunity to teach so many young men my trade.

Another man came by the training center one day, and told me that he was broke. He said that he didn't have any money, but he still had a lot of horses that needed to be shod. He said that I could make up to five thousand dollars, and instead of getting paid in money, I could pick out one of his horses to keep. I told him that I would help him out. I figured that we could accumulate a few horses that way, and Daniel really liked to work with the horses.

We started working for the man, and it didn't interfere with my job at VanVerg's at all. If I had asked Jack, he would have said to go for it.

This meant that Norma would have to quit work, and start training horses again. Norma didn't like the idea of quitting her job, but she did. As I worked, we accumulated two horses and a pony. I knew it would take a little while for Norma to do any good with them, but in the next few months, I was really surprised how well those horses did. Between them, they won several races.

In the winter of nineteen eighty-nine, Norma had gotten two pay horses. Now she had five horses to train. She was stabled in barn one, at Churchill Downs. Churchill had started leaving the barn area open in the winter for training. We had a friend who owned a horse, but was also having some money problems, so we bought his horse for nine hundred dollars.

Daniel and I were helping Norma get the horses out to the track every morning before we went to work. Neil Huffman was stabled in the barn with Norma, and he had a horse that hit worse than any horse I had ever seen. Every morning I walked behind this horse to see if I could figure out, in my mind, what he was doing. Neil had another blacksmith at the time, but I was always trying to find a way to help the horse.

One morning Norma fell in the shedrow, against the tack room door, and broke her shoulder. The doctor told her that she would not be able to work for several months, so Daniel and I would have our hands full, doing Norma's work, and ours, too. Nineteen eighty-nine was an extremely cold winter, so we had to walk the horses in the barn a lot, instead of taking them to the race track. Since I had been working for Jack VanBerg, I didn't have many horses to shoe in the winter at Churchill. It was kind of nice not to be overloaded with work for a change.

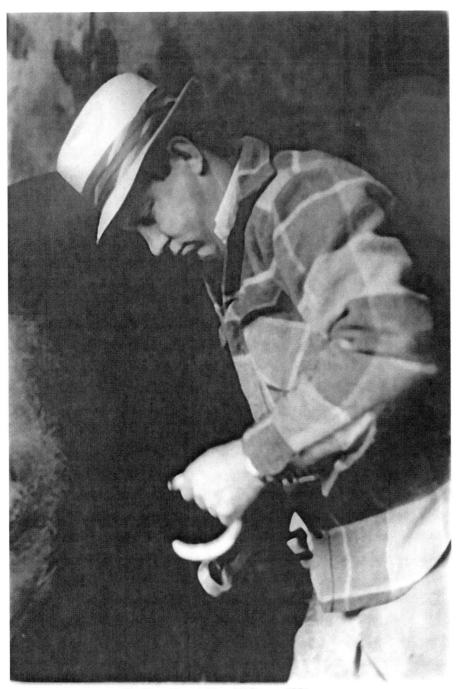

David working at Churchill Downs 1974

In the middle of the winter, Neil Huffman's blacksmith got sick, and had to quit shoeing horses, so Neil asked me if I would start shoeing horses for him. He also said that his brother, Blackie Huffman, would need me to shoe his horses. I had worked for Blackie when he trained horses for Triple R. Farm, and I knew he was a great person. It was amazing how things work out.

I was anxious to shoe the horse for Neil that hit. The horse's name was Fine Point. When Fine Point run in a race, he would run good until midway around the turn, then he would hit his hock so bad that it looked like you took a hatchet to it. After I shod Fine Point, Neil run him again, and he run the same kind of race. He run in to the turn, and hesitated, because he through he was going to hit, but he didn't. He finished third in the race, and that was the first time he had ever hit the board.

Fine Point run at Turfway Park, and I wasn't there to see the race, so I didn't know if he had hit or not, until the next morning. The horse didn't hit, and Neil was tickled to death. We were all happy, but that didn't mean he wouldn't hit the next time he run. When Neil run Fine Point again, he won, and didn't hit again. That is when I knew I had his number.

Fine Point run one more time at Turfway Park, and won again. Neil didn't run him anymore until we got to Churchill Downs. When he run at Churchill, he won again, and somebody claimed him. We didn't see him run again until Ellis Park. The first time he run at Ellis Park, Daniel and I watched the race. His new owner had someone else to shoe him, and he run good until he got halfway around the turn, and then dropped back. I knew that he had hit.

I told my son, Daniel, to go and ask the new trainer if he would sell Fine Point. The trainer wanted to know why we wanted to buy the horse. Daniel said, "my dad knows how to shoe the horse without him hitting". The trainer told Daniel that he wouldn't sell the horse, but he would pay me whatever I wanted to shoe the horse where he didn't hit.

I made arrangements with the new trainer to shoe Fine Point. When I shod him, I had a big audience. By now, I knew how to shoe this horse with no problem. When you shoe a hitting horse, you always have doubts, and can't get careless. In a few days, they run Fine Point again. He finished second, and didn't hit. Before they left Ellis Park, they run him once more, and he didn't hit. He finished third in that race. After the race they sent him to Saint Louis, and I never heard of him again.

A few days later, I started shoeing horses for Neil's brother, Blackie Huffman. It seemed like every stable had at least one hitting horse. Blackie had a real nice horse that had won several stakes races, but he hit real bad when he run. Blackie's son, Ben, told me if I could stop him from hitting, he would be worth a small fortune. The horse's name was Air Worthy, and everyone in the country knew him.

It was still cold weather, so after I shod Air Worthy, it was still a while before Blackie run him in a race. That was good, because it gave me a chance to see how he traveled when he galloped. When Blackie finally run Air Worthy, he didn't hit. I shod Air Worthy for the rest of his racing career, and he won a lot of races.

Over the next several years, Blackie would have multi stake horses. Blackie was a big time trainer, with a smaller stable. In all the years that I worked for him, we never had a problem. If he had a horse that had a problem, and I wanted to talk to him about it, he would say, "you are the blacksmith, shoe him like you would your own". When you work for a trainer like that, you don't have many problems.

Over the years, I learned not to believe all the things that Blackie told me. He was the very best at telling stories. He should be in the story tellers' hall of fame. People like Blackie Huffman don't ever get enough credit. He was a super trainer, and it always gave me a lot of pleasure just telling people that I had to go to Blackie's barn to work.

Another trainer that I always had a lot of respect for, was Donald Hughes. I had been working for Donald for a lot of years, and he had gone from a small stable to a large stable. Donald had a lot of horses with "Peach" in their name, and they were all stake horses. Donald got a horse in his barn one fall, named Lucky Peach. He was running in five thousand dollar claiming races. Donald and I looked at the horse, and he looked bad. I told Donald that it was fall, and he probably needed to be turned out for a couple of months, that it would do him good. After a few days, Donald told me to pull his shoes off, and he would take Lucky Peach to the farm for a while, and turn him out.

When I pulled his shoes off, he had a size four shoe on. Donald left him turned out for two months. When he brought Lucky Peach back to the race track, I put a size seven shoe on him. After Donald got him ready to run again, it was race time. Donald said that he had never seen anything like it. He said that Lucky Peach was working like a stake horse. The first time Donald run him, it was in a high claiming race, and he won, easy. Later on in the Churchill meet, he run the fastest three quarters of a mile, and the fastest mile and a sixteenth, that was run at the meet. Later on Lucky Peach won a few small stake races.

One year at Miles Park, Donald brought a two year old filly to the race track. He said that he wanted me to shoe her, but he would have to tranquilize her first. He said that you couldn't pick up her back feet, because she would try to kick your brains out. When the time come for us to shoe her, Donald said that he was going to the track kitchen to get something to eat. He said to shoe her front feet, and that he would be back by that time, to tranquilize her, to shoe her back feet.

When Donald left, I told Norma to go to the tackroom, and get a set of blinkers. I put the blinkers on the filly so she couldn't see behind her. Usually, when they can't see, they won't kick. I picked up one of her back feet, and she just stood there relaxed, so I put the first back shoe on with no problem. Then I put the second back shoe on with no problem. Then Norma took the blinkers off, and I put the front shoes on. When Donald got back to the barn, he took the filly out of the stall. When he saw that she already had the back shoes on, he said, "No way". He said they had been trying to shoe her all winter, with no luck. For quite a while, when Donald would look at me, he would just shake his head. After a couple of weeks, I told him how we did it. I told him that was an old trick that I learned years before.

A couple of years later, Donald got another filly at the race track, that was the worst I ever saw. She would try to kill you every time you got near her. Her name was Flaming Janie, and they had been galloping her for months, but couldn't touch her back end. She wasn't very good in front, either. Donald told me that we had to get her shod. He set everything up with the vet to tranquilize her. He gave her four cc's of tranquilizer, and it didn't even faze her, so he gave her two more cc's. That didn't do much good either, so he gave her two more cc's. It took over an hour to shoe her.

It was like that every month when we tried to shoe her. She never got much easier all summer.

That fall, Donald decided to go to New Orleans for the winter. I knew they would have trouble in New Orleans, because those blacksmiths wouldn't have as much patience as I did with her.

When winter was over, I was anxious to see what had happened to Flaming Janie. Donald told me that they did get her back shoes off, but couldn't get them back on, so he had to get permission from the stewards to run her without her back shoes on. Donald was glad to see me. She had gotten a lot better, but was still bad.

Donald was a different kind of horseman. He was from the old school, and they did things their own way. Donald was a tough man. I worked for him the better part of thirty years, and there is no telling how many good horses that he has had in his career.

When Norma's shoulder got better, even though she wasn't supposed to do anything for several months, she came back to the race track. She had all those horses, and felt like she should go on with them. Norma and Daniel decided to go to River Downs that summer. The horse that we had bought from Mr. VanBerg won a race at Turfway Park, and had won another race at River Downs.

Norma did really well at River Downs that summer, even though there was a lot of horses that got sick there that year. I thought it would do Daniel good to have a summer off with the horses and his mother, instead of working with me. In the afternoon, Norma and Daniel would go to the races, and make a little extra money, betting on a horse or two.

That fall, after a lot of begging, Norma got a couple of stalls at Churchill Downs. She really didn't have that many horses to run at Churchill, but they all run good. That winter, Jack VanBerg had the stall man to put Norma in the barn with them, at Turfway Park. Jack had thirty horses there, and he always tried to help Norma, and make sure she had enough stalls. Sometimes when you first start to train horses, there is a problem getting stalls.

It has been unreal the way that things worked out. I thank the Lord every day for all the good luck that I've had in my life. I always thought that when I got to a stopping point as a blacksmith, I would like to train some horses, but I realize that will never happen. The next best thing was to watch my wife and kids do well with them. After a couple of years, Norma did so well with the horses, she could get stalls anywhere. I know that Jack VanBerg was a big part of my success. He was the leading trainer in the country, and when you work for a trainer like Jack, everybody wants you to shoe their horses.

When we started hearing rumors that Jack might sell the training center, I thought it wasn't true. That had been my very best job for fourteen years, but as the months went by, it got more real. I was never worried about not having enough work, but I hated to see Jack sell out. He was such a good person to work for, but time changes everything.

When the day come to sell the training center, I went to the race track, and made my rounds. I didn't schedule any work that day, because I wanted to get back to the training center, and be there if they needed any help. I knew it would be hard on Jack, because he was going to be the auctioneer. I bought some lawn furniture, and a few other things at the sale. It was a very long day.

When Van Berg Training Center was going big, it was such a big operation that it was hard to keep up with everything. We had a young man from Iowa to come there, who wanted to be a jockey. His name was Terry Thompson, and he was a very nice young man. When he started working, he had to start from the bottom and work his way up. It is really hard when you start a job with no training. You get all the bad jobs. When anything extra comes up, you get the job.

Every day when I got to the farm to shoe the horses, I had a regular horse holder, but every once in a while, Terry would have to hold a horse or two for me. He did everything well, and he was almost too polite to be around the race track. One of the things that made him tough, was that he raced motorcycles.

Terry caught on quick to riding horses, and he stayed at the farm for the better part of three years. After working at the farm this long, he was ready to go to the race track. Terry and my youngest son Daniel, who helped me every day, had been learning at the same time. Over the years, they had gotten to be good friends.

Norma had six horses in training at Turfway Park, so when Terry wanted to start riding races, he went to Turfway and started galloping horses in the mornings for her. Norma introduced Terry around, and he had such a good personality, that it didn't take long before some of the other trainers started asking him when he was going to start riding races.

Terry got an agent, T. Red Berness, who used to be a good jockey, himself. Norma set up a horse in the second race at Turfway for Terry to ride. By Terry having an agent, it made it all legal. When Terry rode his first race, just like most first time riders, they just hang on, and try to get the horse back safely.

It took a few races for Terry to get the hang of it, and I think he tried too hard for Norma, but after he started riding other horses, it didn't take him long to break his maiden. That is a big deal for a jockey. That is when their career officially starts, with that first win.

In the months ahead, Terry started riding a lot of horses, and was doing well for a young rider. His mother would come to see him ride every once in a while, and we got to know her. She was a very nice lady.

After we bought our house that was next door to Van Berg Training Center, Terry and his mother would come to our house every year for Thanksgiving dinner. Over the years, Terry has been leading rider at a lot of different race tracks. My son, Daniel, and Terry are still good friends.

I never quit working at the training center. The man who bought it, Mike Shutte, had a few horses, and he rented stalls to other trainers, most of whom I worked for. It was never like the old owner. Jack could walk into a barn, and light up a dead frog.

After the training center was sold, it seemed like I still had those lucky ways. It wasn't long until Tony Reinsteddler asked me if I could shoe his horses. He had one of the biggest stables at Churchill Downs. Tony was a young trainer who had been very successful. My first apprentice, John Rosenberg, had been doing Tony's shoeing, until John passed away at forty-four, with a bad heart.

I liked working for Tony. He always had several Derby caliber horses, and he was stabled just two barns down from Blackie Huffman's barn. I could shoe the horses that I had to do for them, and then go to the other end of the race track where most of the other people I worked for was stabled. Norma was stabled in the barn that she had always been in with VanBerg. It still didn't seem natural, for other people to be in Jack's old stalls.

Norma was stabled at Turfway Park that fall, and one of Jack VanBerg's former owners, wanted her to claim, and train, a horse for him. Norma picked out a mare for him to claim, for thirteen thousand and five hundred dollars. The day they claimed the mare, she run at Churchill Downs, and finished third. Norma took the mare back to Turfway Park, and when she run the mare back, she run her for seventeen thousand and five hundred dollars, and won easy. Norma never run the mare again in a claiming race. She started running in allowance races and won several more races in her racing career. Norma had claimed another filly earlier in the summer for fifteen thousand dollars, and she wound up earning almost a hundred thousand dollars. It was amazing how many cheap horses that Norma got in her stable, that turned out to be nice horses.

One weekend, when I was at Turfway Park visiting Norma, I was walking in her barn, and someone said "Mr. Wilson, I have been trying to talk to you." She introduced herself as Barbara Holbrook, and said that she had a few nice horses which needed my attention. She said that she had heard a lot about me, and wanted to know if I would shoe her horses. I told her that I came to Turfway a couple of times a week, and I would be glad to shoe her horses.

After I started shoeing horses for Barbara, it was the start of a long friendship. Sometimes when I would shoe a horse for Barbara, Norma would be with me. I would tell Barbara some kind of big tale, and she would look at Norma to see if it was true or not. Barbara was shy and quiet, and she really liked Norma.

Most of the blacksmiths around the race tracks didn't work on Monday, so after VanBerg left Kentucky, I was free on Monday to go wherever Barbara was stabled, to shoe her horses. She didn't always stable in Kentucky. She went to Hoosier Park and Indiana Downs in Indiana, and River Downs, in Ohio.

Barbara and her husband were both horse trainers. They had some problems in their marriage, and they got a divorce. A little while after their divorce, Barbara had gotten several good horses to train, and I think her ex-husband was jealous of her. One day Norma and I was at Turfway Park, and Barbara had won a big stake race. She said she wanted to give me a stake for shoeing the horse, so she gave me four hundred dollars.

While Barbara was talking to Norma, she told her that she thought her ex-husband was going to kill her, but she didn't know when or where. Of course, we never thought that would actually happen. A few days later, our oldest son, David Jr., called our house. When Norma answered the phone, he asked her if she was sitting down. He told her that Barbara Holbrook's ex-husband had shot her seven times in the back, and killed her. The news of Barbara's death really hurt Norma. I had worked for Barbara for fourteen years, and this really shook me up.

In nineteen ninety-six, a while before Barbara was killed, the house beside the training center where I worked for VanBerg, was put up for sale. Norma was at Turfway Park with the horses, so I bought the house before she ever saw it. When it was time to sign the papers on the house, Norma came home. The lady from the bank told Norma the house looked like "Green Acres", and when our son, Daniel, saw the house, he said we should burn it down, but I saw it differently.

It took a long time to build everything, and remodel the house. The next year, Norma told me that she was getting tired of always being away from home, on the road with the horses. She said that she wanted to be at home for the grandkids. We enjoyed working on our house. Norma might be a woman, but she worked like a man.

It took a while for Norma to get rid of our horses. She sold the ones that we owned, and the owners that she trained for, either sold their horses, or got another trainer. It was such a joy to have Norma home. We had everything turned upside down, and there wasn't much she could do, until all the inside things were done in the house.

I asked Norma if she would like to go with me every day, to help me. I told her that we could plan on everything we were going to do to the house. I got to depend on her. She carried my shoeing box, handed me my shoeing tools, and went to the truck and got the shoes that I put on the horse. It just seemed easier to work with Norma helping me. Norma had such a good personality, and she knew all the people that I worked for. If for some reason she couldn't go to the race track, everyone would say, "where is Norma, we thought she would be here".

We were getting older, and since Norma had quit training, I was trying to cut back some on my work. Between Blackie Huffman, and Tony Reinstedler, they both had several nice allowance horses, and a few stake horses. It was such a pleasure to be involved with trainers with that kind of horses. I had just about the right amount of work.

Even though I had cut back on my work, I still went to River Downs every Monday to shoe horses for my good friend, Jim Morgan, who had about twenty horses in his stable. Also, Kim Chapman, who used to work for Norma, had started training horses. I started shoeing her horses on my days at River Downs.

In the next few years, things didn't change very much. We went to work together every day at the race track, and when we got home, we worked on some project, together. We had a neighbor who helped us some. He would lend me his bobcat when I needed it. It was nice having that kind of equipment right next door.

One day at the race track, I run in to one of the sharpest trainers that I had ever worked for. His name was Jerry Smith, and he had several horses with foot problems. It seemed like everything I did for him was right. In the few years that I worked for him, he made a lot of money with the horses. Jerry stabled his horses in New Orleans in the winter. So did Tony Reinstedler, and Paul MaGee. One of Jerry's owners would pay our expenses, and Norma and I would drive down every month and shoe their horses. We really enjoyed that.

I don't think things could have been better. I had accomplished a lot in the last several years. Maybe not in money, but as a good blacksmith. I had learned so much through experience. A lot of things that I learned was from my sons. Now I know what "time changes everything" means.

In the fall of two thousand, when the Breeder's Cup come to Churchill Downs, they put Scotty Schoffer in the same barn as Tony Reinstedler. Mr. Schoffer had Lemon Drop Kid. He was a two year old, and was going to run in the Breeder's Cup. Tony introduced me to Mr. Schoffer. He told me that Lemon Drop Kid would have to be shod in a couple of days. He said that he would let me know, so that I could take a little extra time on shoeing him, because he was a nice horse.

I always paid special attention when shoeing the big horses, as most of them have a different personality. We got him shod, and he was nice to work on. Mr. Schoffer told me that they would be pleased if he just run good in the Breeder's Cup. He said that Lemon Drop Kid wasn't as mature as most horses at this age. He did run good in the Breeder's Cup, and when Mr. Schoffer left Churchill Downs that fall, he told me to reserve a spot for him when they come back to Churchill the next spring for the Derby.

Churchill meet was over the day after Thanksgiving, and I had to start getting all those horses in order before they started shipping to New Orleans. Every month was like being on a working vacation. We always stayed at the Land Mark Hotel.

On one trip, Norma forgot to take me some dress socks. We went to a clothing store downtown, and while she went in, I was sitting in the car eating a hamburger. The windows on the car were down, and a sea gull swooped down, and took the hamburger right out of my hand. I said to myself, "I hope nobody was watching".

We only had to make three trips every winter. When we would get home, I always had to go to Turfway Park to work. It was a cold place, especially coming out of the warm weather. Since they had put a training facility at the Sports Spectrum, in Louisville, Kentucky, I had several small stables there that I worked for. The weather was always a problem. It is hard to train horses in the winter. You can race, easier than you can train. That's just the way it is.

It didn't take long before spring started popping through. I was looking forward to the Derby. I looked in the paper regularly for Lemon Drop Kid. If you shoe the good ones, you pay more attention to how they run. Keeneland was always a short meeting, and then the "big" horses start moving into Churchill. I liked all the news people with the cameras. I think it is a neat time. If you feel bad all winter, when Derby time rolls around, you automatically feel super.

When Mr. Schoffer shipped in to Churchill, he had five horses in his stable. Lemon Drop Kid sure looked good. They put him in one of the Derby barns, which have a lot of security. The day come for me to shoe Lemon Drop Kid, and I was working on his left front foot. Mr. Schoffer was talking to the owner of Lemon Drop Kid on the cell phone, and I heard him say, "he is working on that foot now". When I heard him say that, I knew that something was up.

Fortunately, I found what they wanted to hear. It looked like the horse had stepped on a board that had a nail in it, and the nail had gone into the horse's foot, but it had healed from the quick out, and was no longer a danger of being sore. Mr. Schoffer was pleased about that. As the week went on, I shod the rest of his horses.

As it got closer to the Derby, I was thinking about all the Derby parties at Churchill. When Norma was training horses, she had a Derby party at the barn every Derby Day. Now that she was no longer training, our son, Daniel, took over doing the Derby parties. Nothing really changed, because Daniel always helped with the cooking, anyway. The only difference was, that now Daniel paid for everything, instead of Norma.

My sister, Betty, and her husband, Allan, had never been to the races. I thought it might be a good time for them to come, since I was involved with a Derby horse. They came to our house, and stayed all night, and then they rode to Churchill with Norma, on Derby day. I drove my truck in case I needed to shoe a horse. When everyone got there, and started eating, my sister had never seen anything like that before. Everyone needs to go to the Derby on the backside of Churchill at least one time in their life.

About 10 o'clock, I made my rounds to check on the horses that I had running that day. There was several horses that I had shod, that was running in other races that day. Just one Derby horse. I asked my sister and brother-in-law if they would like to go with me to make my rounds. I always made my rounds on Derby day by walking to the barns. If anyone needed anything, I would have to go back and get my truck.

Anyway, we made the trip on foot, and so far, there was no problems. When we got to Mr. Schoffer's barn, the groom led Lemon Drop Kid out on the grass for me to check his shoes. My sister had her camera, and she took a picture of me while I was checking him. Everything was OK, so I shook Mr. Schoffer's hand, and wished him good luck. He thanked me for doing his blacksmith work. My sister had a hard time getting over how much money the horses are worth, and how smooth everything runs. It was like clock work.

When it was finally time for the Derby to run, Lemon Drop Kid got hung five horses wide the whole race. If he had had some racing luck, he might have won the Derby. There is a lot of things that can happen with twenty horses running in a race. Mr. Schoffer, and his owners, were satisfied. Lemon Drop Kid wound up being a super race horse. The following year, he was the Eclipse Award Winner. Every time I picked up a racing form to look at the big races, I saw Lemon Drop

Kid's name, not knowing that he would be the last, really good horse, that I would work on.

Now we were enjoying the fruits of our work. We had finished our place a couple of years back. I had a blacksmith shop, second to none. Our yard and flower garden was awesome. We built a picnic area, that you can't imagine what it looked like. There were people who wanted to have weddings, and graduation parties there. We would have probably did this, but we didn't have any outside bathrooms. I was in the process of doing that, but no matter how good things are, there is always bad things that happen.

We had been to Churchill Downs that day, and all the blacksmiths were at the blacksmith shop, just talking, and telling jokes. Everybody seemed to be fine. On his way home, David Woods started feeling bad. He pulled off the road, and called his brother, Charley. Charley called the ambulance, and they got David to the hospital in just a few minutes. I guess that might have saved his life. That night, the doctors only gave David a 10% chance of living, and it was like that for several days. His aorta had burst, which is usually deadly, but he made it through that, and lived.

There was several of us blacksmiths, who split up David's work, and did it for him. We didn't know if he would ever be able to work again. I guess only time would tell. When I picked up the extra work, I didn't know it would be the straw that broke me down.

Everything seemed to be going fine, until I woke up one morning at 3 a.m., and my right hand was numb. I woke Norma up, and she fixed me some coffee. In just a little while, my hand was OK, but I noticed that my eyes weren't focusing right. I wound up at Jewish Hospital, in Louisville, Kentucky. They did numerous tests, and found that my carotid artery in my neck was 95% blocked. They operated on my neck, and I was in the hospital for a week, and then went home.

I decided to walk on the treadmill to get some exercise. On the third day, when I was walking, it felt like a giant rubber band had hit me in the back. Norma was cooking supper, and I had a hard time making it back to the kitchen. I had no idea what had happened. In a few hours,

I started getting electrical shocks in my back. When it did that, I would just freeze in my tracks.

In the next few days, I tried to go to work. When I bent over to try to shoe a horse, it shut my air off. I couldn't figure out why I couldn't breathe. After a few days, I had an x-ray of my back, but it didn't show anything. I heard a nurse say that the film was bad, but they charged me five hundred dollars anyway. The next day my doctor got me set up for a MRI at the University of Louisville Hospital. When the doctor read me the results, it nearly scared me to death. He said my working days were over.

The doctor said that my lower disc and pelvis had deteriorated, and that I would have to do a lot of therapy to hold my back together. He said that I would be totally disabled. What a shock that was. I couldn't help take care of our flowers, or yard work. We had so much, it would take a full time gardener to take care of everything.

We took our time thinking about what to do. This had come about two years too early for me. I had set it up where everything would be paid off in a couple of years. We finally decided to sell our place. We didn't have much choice, the shape I was in, and Norma couldn't take care of everything by herself.

Norma and I went to the Home Depot to get two for sale signs. On the way home, Norma remembered that Mary Lowary had told us if we ever wanted to sell our place to let her know. When we got home, it was late afternoon, and we called Mary. She said that she would be right up to our house.

When Mary got to our house, she brought a real estate contract with her. She left the contract, and said that she would pick it up the next morning. Norma filled the contract out, and Mary picked it up the next morning. She signed the contract and never questioned the price. We had thirty days to move out. I couldn't believe a person could sell a place so quick. I wanted to live there forever, but sometimes things just don't work out the way you want them to. If I hadn't become ill, I would have worked until I fell over.

After we sold our place, we moved into a two bedroom apartment in LaGrange, Kentucky. We had five buildings full of things outside, and a lot of things in the house, that we didn't have room for, so we had a huge yard sale. Our friends and neighbors bought a lot of things, and our son, Daniel, bought some of my tools and yard equipment. We sold almost everything in the yard sale, and the rest, including my blacksmith tools, we put in storage.

When we finally got moved, it was vary hard for me to live in an apartment, knowing that I would never shoe another horse. The doctor told me that I would have to do a lot of therapy, to keep the muscles in my back strong enough to hold it together, so Norma and I joined the YMCA. I started doing water aerobics, and some therapy on the exercise machines. At the time I started, I could barely walk in and out of the YMCA.

I didn't wear socks, because I couldn't put them on. Norma took me to Wal-Mart every day, and I would get a grocery cart to walk with. I couldn't walk very far before I would have to sit down, because I couldn't breathe. It took about two years before I could breathe normal, and nearly three years, before I could walk very well. I never gave up. I had the same heart then, as I did when people used to tell me that I couldn't shoe horses.

In nineteen ninety six, our daughter Terry gave me a paint set for Christmas. I painted a picture of one of our horses, and it looked so good, that it scared me. I tried to paint again in two thousand four, but I just couldn't. I was too nervous. By two thousand six, I had gotten a lot better, so we moved into a house.

The house was close to the street, and there was a lot of people who walked up and down the street in front of our house every day. They would wave and talk to me, and I think that helped me to get better. At least I could think better.

After we had lived there for a while, I got my paint set out and started painting again. I painted twenty-five paintings that year, and did a lot of craft work.

Every summer LaGrange has an arts and craft show on the courthouse lawn. It is called, "Arts On the Green". I sent pictures of my paintings, and crafts that I had made as a blacksmith, to their committee. In a few days I received a letter saying I had been accepted to the art show.

Norma and I bought a gazebo for my booth. Our daughter, Tracy, made flower arrangements for the booth, and it was beautiful. Our other daughter, Tammy, helped around the show with Norma and me. Our daughter, Terry, is the one who bought me my first paint set. I don't know how I got so lucky. All our children are so talented. We have been blessed many times over.

After "Arts On The Green" I got such a response from people who thought I was just a blacksmith. Even the other artists told me that I have a unique way of painting. Being a blacksmith is an art, in itself, and I really enjoy what I do. It's fun to paint the picture, and then make the frame to hang it in. Our youngest daughter, Tina, lives in South Carolina, but she, and our other daughters, keep me in art supplies.

A few years earlier, before I had to retire, I was at River Downs Race Track shoeing horses for Jim Morgan. While I was shoeing a horse in the shedrow, a man came by the barn, and was talking to us. The man told me that he had seen my picture, the day before, in the Kentucky Derby Museum. I told the man that I didn't know I had a picture in the museum.

The next day, I was sitting in the blacksmith shop at Churchill Downs, and another blacksmith came in. He told me that he had taken his kids to the Kentucky Derby Museum, and they saw my picture on the wall. I asked him what size the picture was, and he said "about the size of your truck". I told Norma that I thought they were all lying to me, but maybe we should go to the museum, and check it out. To my surprise, there was an eight foot square picture of me, shoeing a horse. I couldn't believe my eyes.

After I couldn't shoe horses anymore, because of my health, I told Norma that was where my tools should be, right under my picture in the museum. I called the museum, and talked to Jay Fergerson about donating my tools. After Mr. Fergerson found out who I was, he said the museum would be glad for me to donate my tools. On February 17, 2006, a news conference was called, so that I could present my tools to the museum. All the local television stations were on hand to televise the presentation.

In two thousand eight, Norma's fiftieth high school class reunion was held in Lebanon, Kentucky. That is where we all went to high school. Me, and five of my friends, decided to quit school and conquer the world. I had kept in touch with one of my friends, Bobby Isham, over the years, and every once in a while he would call me.

A few weeks before the reunion, Bobby called me, and asked what I thought about all us boys getting together again. He said that we could talk about when we were young, and gathered at the Lebanon Fair Grounds to discuss what we were going to do for the day. The fair grounds was our headquarters, and we gathered there to discuss everything.

The reunion was held in a motel in Lebanon, so I told Bobby that would be a good time for us to get together. Bobby called everyone else, and let them know what we wanted to do. Norma and I stayed at the motel on Saturday night, where the reunion was held.

Arts on the Green

David working on Murry the last horse he shod 2004

On Sunday morning, Bobby brought Orville Walls out to the motel. They picked me up, and we went to see Roger Thompson. Roger had fallen and broke his hip a few months before that, but was doing fine. Morris Glazebrook was not able to come, because of bad health. We went to the Cedar Wood Restaurant, in Lebanon, and ate lunch, and talked for quite a while. I couldn't believe how good everyone looked, and how well everyone had done, after all these years. It certainly was a wonderful day.

On the morning of the flood in Louisville, Kentucky, in May 2009, I was watching television, and could not believe my eyes. The water in the parking lot at the Kentucky Derby Museum was so high, that all you could see was the tops of the cars. Everything in sight was covered in water. I could not believe that so much water could accumulate in that area.

There had been times when I was working at Churchill Downs, and the drains would back up, and there might be two or three feet of water in the barn area, but this water rose so quickly, that it was impossible to believe.

I can't imagine what the people who work in the museum were going through. They were trying to move everything to a higher floor. My blacksmith tools that I had donated to the museum was in a glass case on the ground floor, so I knew that they were covered with water. The worst part it wasn't just rain water, it was sewer water.

For the next several weeks, I didn't do anything. I guess that I didn't want to hear that my lifetime of making, and collecting, my tools were destroyed.

I go to the YMCA three times a week, and each time I was there someone would ask me what had happened to my tools. After a few weeks I finally decided to call Lynn Ashton, who is the executive director of the Derby Museum. It was so odd, because when I dialed the phone, Lynn Ashton was the one who answered the phone, and it didn't even ring.

I was completely stunned, but I told her who I was, and that I was concerned about my tools. Mrs. Ashton assured me that they were safe and sound. Also dry.

If I could live my life over again, I wouldn't change a thing. I hope who ever reads this book, enjoys reading about my life, as much as I enjoyed living it.

David Wilson

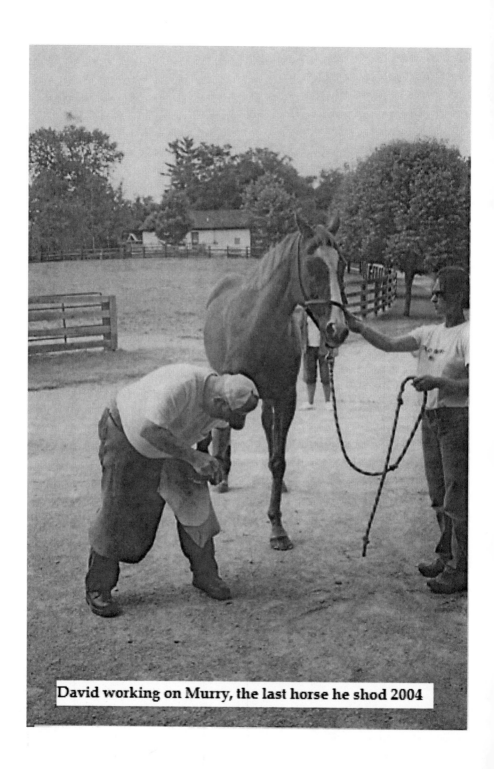

David working on Murry, the last horse he shod 2004

MUSEUM ACQUIRES TOOLS FROM
LEGENDARY FARRIER

Media Advisory: **Contact: Courtney Stinson Mangeot**
                                        Public Relations Manager
                                        Kentucky Derby Museum
                                        (502) 992-5910
                                        Cell : (502) 693-5605

Louisville, Ky. (February 16th, 2006)- The *Kentucky Derby Museum* is proud to announce the acquisition of farrier David Wilson's rare toolbox and tools. Wilson, an expert farrier at Churchill Downs for over 50 years, will be present during a special presentation on **Friday, February 17, 2006 at 10:30 am at the Kentucky Derby Museum.**

"Mr. Wilson's generosity will allow us to showcase artifacts along with props. They will bring a new dimension and broaden the history of our exhibit and allow us to share the stories that these pieces lived," states Lynn Ashton, Executive Director of the Kentucky Derby Museum.

Wilson, who has worked with racing legends such as trainer James "Sunny Jim" Fitzsimmons and jockey Bill Hartack, has shoed some of racings most notorious horses. The tools and apron that he used during his career are being generously donated to the Kentucky Derby Museum to further educate visitors on the process of shoeing and the importance of the backside workers.

Among the items being donated is a rare toolbox, one-of-a-kind apron and clinching block. The aluminum toolbox that Wilson is donating to the Museum was the first of only forty made. The apron is an innovative design created by Wilson. Magnets were sewn into the apron to hold the nails so that he would not have to hold them in his mouth while working with a horse. The tool box holds a wonderful collection of tools that date back to 1970 and were used by Wilson to shoe racing legends such as 1987 Kentucky Derby winner **Alysheba.**

##

The Kentucky Derby Museum is a non-profit organization dedicated to expanding public awareness, appreciation, and understanding of the evolution and meaning of the Kentucky Derby. The Kentucky Derby museum is located at Gate 1 of Churchill Downs. Admission is $9 for adults, $8 for seniors, $4 for children 5-11, and children under 5 are free. Museum is open from 9 a.m.-5 p.m. Monday-Saturday, and noon-5 p.m. on Sunday, closed Thanksgiving, Christmas, Oaks, Derby and Breeders' Cup days. For additional information pertaining to the Kentucky Derby Museum and Membership opportunities please visit www.derbymuseum.org.

#

SHELBY
EQUINE
ASSOCIATES, P.S.C.

5898 Aiken Road
Louisville, KY 40245

6SEP07

Assuming no negative in the term "salt of the earth" ,that's how I think of my long-term friend David Wilson.He has always been the very representation of a great farrier and American to me.

In my opinion, there never has been a better farrier. Many times over the last couple of decades I've sought David's advice for patient's shoeing problems. Especially , he has always been "the man " to stop a horse from" hitting"; that means that the horse may be "cross-firing", interfering ,over-reaching , forging ,or whatever.Horsemen want to know why the horse was hitting, and what it took to correct the problem. David was never into lengthy, unnecessary analysis."What did you do David ?" The usual answer was "Oh , I just shod him right".

David's son Daniel has followed in his footsteps; predictably enough, Daniel is as good as you'll find. He's not excited about shoeing racehorses; he's the best around at event or dressage or hunter/jumpers or whatever he gets under.

Although I've met David Jr. , I know nothing about his work , but I'll bet he's good at it.

Sincerely,

Oscar Swanstrom, DVM

GLENWOOD
VETERINARY
SERVICES

Practice Limited to Horses

RICHARD J. COSTELLE, D.V.M.
P.O. Box 263 • Sellersburg, IN 47172-0263
Home: (502) 893-8381
Mobile: (502) 551-9786

January 7, 2008

To Whom It May Concern:

As a current practitioner on the Kentucky horse racing circuit, I would like to take a moment to interject on the career of Mr. Wilson, a prominent Kentucky blacksmith. I call him "Mr. Wilson" because that is how he was introduced to me, and I've never heard of him being referred to in any other way. I think that speaks volumes to the integrity of his craft, and to the respect that Kentucky horsemen have of him, and of his family. I have interacted on many occasions with Mr. Wilson; his wife, Norma, a trainer; and his son Daniel, also a blacksmith. When a racehorse needs shoeing, there are plenty of blacksmiths to call, but when a horse's feet need to be fixed, call Mr. Wilson.

Sincerely,

R. Costelle DVM

F. P. Sprinkle, M.S. D.V.M.
Equine Practioner
P.O. Box 276
Buckner, Kentucky 40010
(502) 363-1299

Like a lot of us, David Wilson has had several different jobs working around horses. I have heard his stories of working as an exercise rider at Claiborne Farm and negotiating with Bull Hancock for additional pay for himself and the other riders. I came to know him as a farrier at Churchill Downs. He would gather his tools and apron, sit a little while, tell a story, listen and laugh at some else's big tale, then quietly go about his work. Now those hands that so deftly trimmed, balanced and shod the hooves of countless horses, tend full time the garden; where his goal has always been to have the first and biggest ripe tomatoes of the summer and work in the wood shop putting the finish on a hand crafted piece. His work here will reflect that same kind of attention.

F. P. Sprinkle MS DVM

December 6, 2007

Workbook Pages

Churchill Downs
Van Berg Stable
1991

Nov 4	Run In my Stocking	4 New pads	$50
5	Uptown Skirt	4 New pads	"
14	Hawkins Buddah	4 New pads	"
	Somethingotagine	4 New Pads	"
15	Rallys Luck	4 New pads	"
	Alyoni	4 New	65.00
18	Nyacmas of U	4 New pads	35.00
	National Fashion	4 New pads	"
19	Heres to you Slew	4 New pads	"
22	Derby Deal	4 New pads	"
	Monsterrat	4 New pads	"
	1st Issue	4 New pads	"
23	Oct Mc Geisler	4 New pads	"
	Pony	4 New	
25	Taunch A Ruler	4 New pads	"
26	Jamies Revenge	4 New pads	"
	Maria Jesse	4 New pads	"
27	Dexter	4 New Pads	"
	To Hane	4 New pads	"
29	unlikely Story	4 New pads	"
	Foyt Five Hundred	4 New pads	"
	Big Gate	4 New pads	"
30	Stronger every day	4 New pads	"
			1585.00

Neil Huffman

Nov 7 Seven Spades 4 Whirpools

Paramount Farm Std

Nov 1 Sagme   2 New train
    11 Bankers Spirit   4 Whir Swords
    21 Szaber   2 New train
        Xcelant   2 New train
        Blythmorgana Copy 2 New train
        Amicah   2 New train
        Kakemier   2 Whir train
        Szkana   2 New train
        Pritben   2 New train
                        _____
                        365. 00

W. G. Huffman

1993

Oct 5	Wabi Warrior	4 Mew	70.00
	Devils Hunch	4 Mew	"
12	Loving Cutthroat	4 Mew	"
13	Smile	4 Mew	"
15	Durham	4 Mew	"
18	Gotta Groove Grover	4 Mew	"
21	Coach Harper	4 Mew	"
22	Teddy's Turn	4 Mew	"
24	What A Wabi	4 Mew	"
25	Danville	4 Mew	"
27	Missy	4 Mew pads	$5.00
29	Medley	4 Mew	

785.00

Neil Huffman

Oct 19   Honey N Ice   4 Thio pads
     26   Hyper Shu   4 Thio pads

                                  ———
                                  140.⁰⁰

J. E. Morgan

Oct 25   true Memories   4 Thio
         Rip Dabbs 70⁰⁰   4 Thio pads
         Quartan Acids   ———
                                  135.⁰⁰

Barbara Holbrook

1		Diamond Affair	Backle 25.00
2	July 5	Payrant E la	2 New + Trim
3	12	Diamond Affair	4 New + Mitts
4	15	Quiz Question	4 New
5	19	Enchanted Dreamer	4 New
6		Chief Rainbow	4 New
7	22	Mabel's Love	2 New + Trim
8	29	Not New Maybe Later	2 New + Trim
9			
10			2/450.00
11			
12	Aug 9	~~Diamond Affair~~	
13			
14			
15			
16			
17			
18			
19			
20			
21			
22			
23			
24			
25			
26			

Page 202

Barbara Holbrook
Pd 160.00

June	23	Halls Hill Road		2 New & Drum
		Saint Golddigger		2 New & Prim
Aug	1	St Golddigger		4 New
		Stepintothefire		4 New
		Polish Snoop		4 New
	7	J. No Mad Broom		4 New
		Halls Hill Road		2 New Prim
		Sheikworthpleasure		4 New
	15	Malang		4 New
		Chelsie		4 New
			pd	760.00

Anthony Reinstedler
1999

Date	Name		
June 4	Ally Blue	2 New	45.00
5	Frozen Chosen	4 New	80.00
	Mr Williams	2 New	
8	Brittywood	4 New	
9	Ygathan	4 New	
	Clovering Monarc	2 New	
	tawa Keen	2 New	
11	Stateliness	4 New	
	Miss Barbara	4 New	
12	St Finnin	4 New	
	Mr Williams	2 New	
15	Pyrenne	4 New	
	Ygathan	2 New	
18	Blue Sky Blue	4 New	
	Celestral Crown	4 New	
19	Clenardar	4 New	
	Post Code Colt	4 New	
22	Longuist Moor (ule) Colt	4 New	
27	Dimmers on Me	4 New	
	Bullett Buzz	4 New	
29	Ygathan	2 Dest	30
30	Clenardar	4 New	
			$1470.00

W.C. Huffman
1992

June	4	Degree	4 New	65.00
	12	Vanlandinghamcolt	4 New	"
		Little Current Filly	4 New	"
	19	Groovy Colt	4 New	"
		Sweet Nature,	4 New	"
		Walsh Worrier	3 New	"
	20	Stormbird Colt	4 New	"
	23	Cato Double Colt	4 New	"
	24	Air Worthy	4 New	"
		Cut the Ressin	4 New	"
	26	Action In Motion	4 New	"
		Ephmen	4 New	"
	29	Whiskey	4 New	"
		Poisonous	4 New	"
		Devils Punch	4 New	"
	30	Some Catch	4 New	"

1009.50

Pat Huffman
2004

June	4	Gunther Colt		4 New	100.00
		Eye of The Tiger		4 New	"
		Steel Curtain		4 New	"
	7	Dance To Dawn		4 New	"
		Molta Vita		4 New	"
		Price Discovery		4 New	"
	11	Storm Boot Filly		4 New	"
		Initial		4 New	"
		Storm Bird Colt		4 New	"
	12	Jostlin Kate		2 New + Rim	55.00
		Purple Hill		4 New	100.00
		Tempered Steel		4 New	"
	13	Dinner's On Me		4 New	"
		Smithie		4 New	"
		Aiken Drum		2 New + 2 Drum	50.00
	14	Deputy Commander ✓		4 New	100.00
		Seattle Slew		4 New	"
		De Hare		4 New	"
	19	Ice Forest		4 New	"
		Queen Mindy ✓		4 New	"
		Dance Apollo		4 New	"
	21	Rhino		4 New	"
		Kappa House		4 New	"
	25	Urban Distraction ✓		4 New	"
		Spurred On		4 New	"
		Jenny's Jewel		4 New	"
	28	Paul's Cat ✓		4 New	"
				Pd 2120.00	
		Kuehne		Pd 500.00	

Van Berg Farm
1989

Feb 26	Special Butler	4 New	60	00
	My First Ego	2 New trim	34	00
	Family til too	2 New trim	34	00
	Phantom Signal	2 New trim	"	
27	National Fashion	2 New trim	"	
	Run & Win	2 New trim	"	
	Down to Rio	2 New trim	"	
	Aura of Fire	2 New trim	"	
	Review my Record	2 New trim	"	
28	Shop til ten	2 New trim	"	
	Nearness of you	2 New trim	"	
	Something Got to Give	2 New trim	"	
	Young + Flirty	2 New trim	"	
Mar 1	Strode About	2 New trim	"	
	Los Flores Nation	2 New trim	"	
	Running Wonder	2 New trim	"	
	Pop pop's Gold	trim	4	00
2	Ken per Day Gold	2 New trim	34	00
	Welcome to my World	2 New trim	"	
	Darced	2 New trim	"	
			700.	00

P. E. Hughes
1989

Mar	1	Receptionist	4 Thurs	60 00
		Dice Girl	4 Thurs	"
		Lady tanch	4 Thurs	"
	2	Irish Wit	4 Thurs	"
	3	Peaches Best	4 Thurs	
	6	Freeman	4 Thurs pads	65 00
		Face	4 Thurs pads	
	7	Some Hu Honest	4 Thurs pads	
		Ryder	4 Thurs	"
	9	Pony	3 Thurs trip	34 00
	13	Bearlty Cooking	4 Thurs pads	
		Hopeful Duane	4 Thurs	60 00
	14	Chicken Vodka	4 Thurs pads	
	23	Seamon	4 Thurs	
		Moe Prospector	4 Thurs pads	65 00
	26	Lucky Peach	4 Thurs pads	"
	30	Hatchi Hill	4 Thurs pal.	"

1,095 00

James Keefer

Mar	7	Mo Mac	4 Thurs	60. 00

1972

Dr. I. M. Snider

Mar.	10	G. b Forward Thrust	4 New Felt	#26. 00
		2 year old Colt	4 New	22. 00
		2 year old Filly	4 New	22. 00
		Sherry's Gotta Go	4 New	22. 00
		European Tour	4 New	22. 00
	21	G. b Forward Thrust	2 New + Pads	15. 00
		Sue Bigley	Reset 4	16. 00
				#145. 00

Jessie Dixon

Mar. 16	Petite-A-Tole	Reset 4	#16. 00

W. F. Janson

Mar. 13	Hiss Ho	Reset 4	$16. 00

R. C. & L. C. Hughes

Mar. 14	Dawn by Vis Count	4 New	#22. 00
	Sir Ribot Colt	4 New	22. 00
	Speeding Traffic	4 New	22. 00
	Col. Jones	4 New	22. 00
	Maride	4 New	22. 00
15	No Fear Filly	4 New	22. 00
	Admiral Criss	4 New	22. 00
	Delta Dodge	4 New	22. 00
	Miss Pin Couson	4 New	22. 00
			#198. 00

J. Wright

Fire Brewed	4 New	$22. 00

Bill Bruning

Stamped In Blue	4 New	$22. 00
New River	4 Reset	16. 00
		38. 00

Stanley Conrad

Misty Cast	4 New	$22. 00
Stone Wood	4 New	22. 00
		#44. 00

March Work 1972
Morris Fife

Date		Horse	Work	Amount
Mar.	9	Bay Mare	2 New	$10.00
	26	Franklin Jane	4 Reset + Felt	20.00
				$30.00

Fred Wirth

Date		Horse	Work	Amount
Mar.	7	3 year old colt	2 New + Trim	$12.00
	11	Gray at Last	4 New + wedges	24.00
	17	Pony	4 New	20.00
		Front Lass	4 New	22.00
	21	3 year old Colt	2 New + 2 Reset	19.00
	23	Grey at Last	2 Resets wedges	12.00
	31	Beau Prince Colt	4 New	22.00
				$131.00

Joe Marquette

Date		Horse	Work	Amount
Mar.	7	Sir Pompain	Reset 4	$16.00
		Get of on	Reset 4	16.00
		Pony	4 New	16.00
	13	Hurry Home Cindy	Reset 4	16.00
	21	Withered Smoke	Reset 4	16.00
				$80.00

Kennith Burkhart

Date		Horse	Work	Amount
Mar.	13	Play Boy Husband	4 New	$22.00
		Mh. Joe Dee	4 New	22.00
	22	Wise advice	4 New	22.00
		Boom Fellow	Trim	4.00
	27 (23)	Bold Mac	4 New	22.00
	(22)	Can Pretend	4 New	22.00
				$114.00

Page 210

Jan. 1972   Work

Clarence Picue Stable · Fred Bradley

Date	Horse	Work	Amount
Jan. 3	Guide Light	4 New	$20.00
	Voodo Groom	4 New	20.00
	Hayo'n Law	2 Reset	7.50
	Pitau Blue	2 Reset	7.50
Jan. 4	Martian	4 New + Felt	24.00
	Crystalus	4 New	20.00
paid	Double Dollar	Reset 4	15.00
	Rablero Clover	4 New	20.00
	Dodger Colt	Reset 4	15.00
	Middle Ground Filly	Reset 4	15.00
	Father's Image Filly	Reset 4	15.00
			$179.00

Clarence Picue

Jan. 3	Talley Colt	4 New	$20.00
	Smart Filly	Reset 4	15.00
			$35.00

Mr. Jessie Dixon

Jan. 21	Petite-A-tole	Reset 4	$15.00
	Lady Rachel	4 New	20.00
			35.00

Dr. J. M Snider

Jan. 17	2 year old filly	2 New + Trim	$11.00
	2 year old Colt	2 New + Trim	11.00
Jan. 26	European Tour	4 New	20.00
	Sue Bagley	4 New	20.00
			$62.00

Mr. Danny Shearer

Jan. 21	Go Far Bailey	Reset 2	$7.50
	Poker Bow	2 New + Trim	11.00
			$18.50

2

1972   Mr. Arnold Warner
3916 Upper River Rd. Louisville, Ky.

Jan.	31	Arm Up	Trim	$ 4.	00
		Beau Jenny	Trim	4.	00
paid		C maria	Trim	4.	00
		Kingar	Trim	4.	00
		Songatar	Trim	4.	00
		Misty Miracle	Trim	4.	00
		Arma Sub	Trim	4.	00
		Go Go	Trim	4.	00
				$32.	00

Dr. Alex Harthill

Jan.	3	Groton filly	2 New + Trim	$11.	00
paid		Ap th filly	2 New + Trim	11.	00
		Double Jay Gd.	2 New + Trim	11.	00
Jan.	2	Gay Wilhemine	2 New + Trim	11.	00
		Maddie filly	4 New	20.	00
Jan.	22	Mr. Gem	2 New + Trim	11.	00
		Bay Filly	2 New + Trim	11.	00
		Pony	Trim	4.	00
		Bay Horse	Trim	4.	00
		Romeo	2 New + Trim	11.	00
		Juliet	2 New + Trim	11.	00
				$116.	00

Mr. F. W. Janson
12112 St Clair Dr. Middletown, Ky.

paid					
Jan.	3	Dia Ko	2 New + Trim	$11.	00

Page 212

CPSIA information can be obtained at www.ICGtesting.com
Printed in the USA
LVOW040509250113

317142LV00001B/5/P